And What Is Hell?

A True Story As Told By Sara Ramsey
And Written By Dorothy Ramsey

Edited by Michael Miller, M.Ed., M.S.

PYRAMID PRESS
9550 South Eastern Avenue • Suite 253
Las Vegas, NV 89123 U.S.A.
contact@pyramidpress.net

And What Is Hell?

A True Story As Told By Sara Ramsey
And Written By Dorothy Ramsey

Edited by Michael Miller, M.Ed., M.S.

Romans 9:9 *For this is the word of promise,*
at this time will I come, and Sarah shall have a son.

PYRAMID PRESS

International Standard Book Number: 10: 0989901769
International Standard Book Number: 13: 978-0-9899017-6-5

First Pyramid Press Edition 2015

The paper used in this publication meets the minimum requirements
of the American National Standard for Permanence of Paper
for Printed Library Materials Z39.48-1984.

Printed in U.S.A.

PYRAMID PRESS
9550 South Eastern Avenue • Suite 253
Las Vegas, NV 89123 U.S.A.
contact@pyramidpress.net

Contents

Luke 2:12 *And this shall be a sign unto you;*
Ye shall find the babe wrapped in swaddling
clothes, lying in a manger.

Insane treatment of the mentally ill and others institutionalized was the norm.

Patton State Hospital – 1900. For years, this institution in San Bernardino County, California, was known only as "The Insane Asylum."

Preface

Few have written of mental hospitals as their main theme, and of the unfortunate inmates incarcerated therein, therefore this story lived many years ago by two people who suffered such a fate, gives true statements of facts. Only true names of people and places are withheld to save relatives of participants sorrow and embarrassment.

To this day, the average person is unaware of the sad plight of the mentally insane, and whose condition and treatment is still shrouded in mystery. They are outcasts, either ignored, laughed and mocked at, or avoided as dangerous creatures by their neighbors. Herded behind bars in public institutions, they were at the time of this story, and perhaps even now, treated and considered as nothing more than animals, incapable of either mental or physical feeling, deprived of every freedom, human right and decency, and used as "guinea pigs" to test each new psychiatric theory.

Why have writers failed to give full and true accounts of the living death suffered by thousands of helpless, mind-sick, innocent living victims? Was it fear of persecution? Was it fear of public opinion? Fear of any kind cannot touch the two who caused this story to be written, for they have passed beyond fear of any kind and beyond further punishment.

The woman who experienced these terrible conditions told me the story when she was an old and tired woman, but whose mind was as keen as in the years of her youth. She often tried to write the story, but poverty and overwork had compelled her to wait. At last fearful that she would fail her *master* and humanity, she told me the story, day by day, as we were together. She told it just as it had occurred; nothing had been forgotten, for the horrors of that time were indelibly impressed in her mind. She did not minimize her breach of the law, freely she admitted it, saying to, "Tell it just as I have told it to you. This will save others from anguish and torment if they will believe that I told it for their sakes."

Her mother heart, big enough to "mother" all the world, was filled with compassion and sorrowful grief as she talked with me. So faithfully as she told it to me, I tell it to all listening humanity who have eyes to see and ears to hear.

This story is dedicated to the lost, downtrodden, discouraged, hopeless. To the drunkards, the harlots, adulterers, and to the rich, who have found no panacea in their riches, no joy in their great possessions.

"Though your sins be as scarlet, I will make them like snow; though they be red as crimson, I will make them as white as wool. I will blot them out and remember them against you no more forever. I will remove them from you as far as the east is from the west." Isaiah 1:18.

When will *he* do this? When you forsake your sins, calling on the *name* of the Lord. You may say, "I do not believe in God." My answer is, that if you had spent only a few days in hell, you would change your mind, "For truly God is in this place."

Again she said to me, "My dear friend, you promised to write every word just as I have told it to you. I thank God for you. You shall not lose your reward."

And it is as she prophesied, I have received a priceless *reward*. Greater than all the earthly treasures of silver and gold, precious beyond expectation, a reward that far surpasses the flights of imagination, incomparable with any material thing. This "great reward" is *spiritual liberty* given by the Lord God *almighty* to all who will believe the *revelation he* gave the women twenty-one years after her release from hell of that most *"holy thing,"* the *gift* of God, *his only begotten son* Jesus Christ.

This story is of a woman who, with all her hungry soul, sought spiritual truth and understanding at the mouths of preachers, teachers, priests of religion, and of lawyers and judges of man's law. The men and women who call themselves ministers of God's *word*, the men of law, none of these could give unto her the truth and understanding of God's *words*. None could tell her the meaning of the *bread* of *heaven*, or the *water* of *life*. Like the prodigal son who would fain have eaten the husks with the swine, but no man gave unto her.

She loved little children devotedly. She said that they were, "Fresh from heaven and God's smile was in their eyes."

Herein is told the beginning of the spiritual struggle of this woman, chosen and called of God, to give up all superstitions, pagan traditions, literal biblical misunderstandings of the old religious world, and the price that was paid in hell for the privilege of afterward pioneering through untold mental and physical hardships to again restore to the perishing world the blessed knowledge of *"the way, the truth, and the life"* of God's *holy words*.

Earnest, true, just men and women and children, the words of this story will open your eyes, will open your souls to lost humanity. You will forget yourselves and remember The God who bought you with *his* own *blood*. Some day, He will *reveal* to you the potency of that *blood*, which has the power to "heal the sick, cleanse the leper, give sight to the blind, and raise the dead."

This world knows the horrors of wars, of prison camps, horrors experienced by thousands to whom death would have been a welcome relief. But even the story of "The Snake Pit" only lightly touches the surface of hell, where *"the smoke of their torment ascendeth up forever."* Revelation 14:11.

Remember the immortal words of Jesus, *"He that is without sin among you, let him first cast a stone at her."* John 8:7.

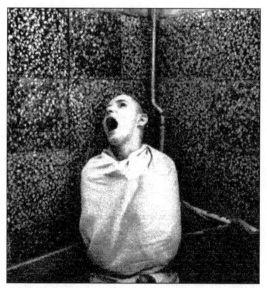

Some individuals who were mentally ill, others incarcerated for being addicts, alcoholics, outcasts, religious zealots, impoverished, and other questionable reasons, experienced horrors—some death, while captive in an insane asylum's padded cells and secret back rooms.

Part I
CALLED BY HIS NAME

HELL

In earth's dark caverns, hidden

From the sunlight's rays,

Blackened by sin and it's curses,

Turned to their many ways;

Souls are waiting for the coming of Jesus,

Who died to save,

Jesus Christ, overcomer of death, hell, and the grave.

The sun gone down and over all,

The horrors, the darkness of midnight's pall,

As in the darkness wild beasts seek their prey,

So in this place of torment, far from life's glad way,

Shrieks, curses, prayers and groans,

Laughter, sorrow, heartbreaking moans.

Cries, loud and long, and anguished tears,
Language vile, pleadings, jeers all intermingle,
While amid the clamor comes a cry,
"Water, water, I thirst, I thirst,
Oh give me water lest I die!"
Is God unmindful of this awful curse?

Will souls forever be in such despair?
What says the *book*? "Yes, though I make my bed in hell,
Yet is *he* there."
Hell hath enlarged her borders,
And deep in pits of sin,
Souls are yet crying for pardon,
And such, *his* love will win.

He holds the key of hell, *immortal one*, is *he*,
Hearest thou not the words?
He'll set the captives free,
He'll break the bands of sin that bind,
He'll wipe all tears away,
     The Savior of all mankind.

CALLED BY HIS NAME

We sat at our meager and tasteless breakfast, and though the food was not nutritious and not enough of it, it was clean. A bare table, bleak surroundings, the surroundings of poverty in the extreme. James and I both had taken the *scriptures* literally, and had given up all our earthly possessions to follow Jesus through darkness and misunderstanding. Humbly, sincerely we did this, not knowing to what it would lead us, and what would be the cost. We knew the reward, but did not know the reward itself.

It was April, near the end of the month. Suddenly the sadness and wonder of the unknown path came to me.

"We must go through hell, to get to heaven," I said for the first time to James.

I did not know what I said, because I had no knowledge of either heaven or hell. According to the teachings of my young childhood, hell was a place under the ground, burning with fire and brimstone, occupied by the devil, his angels, and bad people. If we were bad, we would go down to hell when we died, to be burned in hell forever. But if we were good, we would be carried up into heaven.

Heaven was described as a wonderful place above the sky, with golden streets, crystal rivers, white-robed angels flying around a great white throne on which God sat, with Jesus standing at *his* right hand. Those angels knelt to worship and played on harps of gold. These harps appealed most to my childish mind, for I loved music dearly and music of harps best of all. There are, millions still having that remote picture of heaven today.

The *scriptures* are true, but there is only one way to understand the *scriptures*, and that is by the *spirit* that gave them. "The *scriptures* are of no private interpretation." At that time I did not know. It was true that James and I had to go through hell to get to heaven, to know what you and all the world should know, to understand what it was that God gave to the world when *he gave his only begotten son, and that he gives the same today and forever.* Hebrews 13:18.

Back then when life seemed so much simpler, I was born to poor but honest parents, who taught me the things that I should be proud of were truth, honesty, justice and mercy. A love for all people to whom I should give aid and comfort as much as was possible. This was a good heritage, greater than the heritage of kings and queens. Through my parents, truth was inherent in me and still it is there. But now much multiplied, for I have the *truth* of God's blessed words by *his spirit*.

The first thing I read (after newspapers which Father taught me to read at the age of four) was the Bible. I was too small to carry that great old leather bound Bible, which had belonged to my father's father, so I dragged it and sitting on the floor read and father told me how to say the big words. I did not know then that no one could read it as it should be read, with the *understanding*—not even my father, whom I thought was the best and wisest man in all the world.

My companion of that lowly breakfast had been my companion for several weeks. We read the Bible together from five o'clock in the morning until hours had passed, then we read it again late at night. Constantly we read, and morning, noon and night we knelt in earnest prayer together.

We prayed, "Thy will be done." We prayed for guidance for each day. We prayed that others would believe the *message* of our *father's name revealed* two years before. We prayed for "daily bread," not knowing what that *bread* was. To us then, it was bread to stay our hunger, although God mercifully kept us from being very hungry, only for *him* whom we adored.

For we had no money, except as some listening to the songs given or the words spoken put a dime or quarter into one of our hands. We asked for nothing of money or goods, we had no offering box. James took the meager sums given us and walked miles to a large market, coming back with a few potatoes one day, another perhaps a small loaf of bread or a melon, or some kind of fruit. There was never enough to buy meat, even the cheapest kind.

Each day we walked together to Pershing Square, where street meetings were held to tell the *gospel* story so precious to us. They were long walks, as we had nothing with which to pay for rides. All our friends had forsaken us but two, because we were living together without marriage by the law. We were not ignorant of this; we knew that some day we should meet punishment at the hands of the law, but did not know what that punishment would be.

We believed at that time that the people of God did not need the sanction of the law, for we read in the *scriptures* of the joining of the people of God. We knew that the law married men and women and gave them divorces, afterwards remarrying them to others. We believed true marriage was "until death do you part." We read in the *scriptures*, "Be not conformed to this world, but be ye transformed." We still believe that marriage is holy, sacred, pure, and that death has no power to part the chosen of God.

We were sacrifices for the hidden *truth* which is a mystery to all the world until it is *revealed*. It was not yet *revealed* to James or to me. We had "forsaken all" to follow Jesus and the *disciples* in the way we believed was right for us to take. How many have hoped to find the way to follow Jesus? But did it lead them along the thorny path into the depths of darkness? Did it lead them to where they must drink the bitterness of gall? Yea, to the very dregs?

Did they hear that sweet, still *voice* say, "Will you drink this cup for *me, my* child?"

Did they, in their blindness, answer as I did, "I will, Lord, I will, I will."?

You may say (and think yourselves justified, as thought those who crucified our Lord), "What ignorance!"

We had no knowledge of the things afterwards *revealed* to us. We were now wise in this world's conceits; we were never exalted by thinking ourselves better than anyone else. Following Jesus without *light*, following *him* through darkness so great, so appalling, following *him* with broken heart and blinded eyes. Breaking *his* law and being blind to that fact until *he* opened my eyes. Losing friends and relatives so dear to me, losing reputation, and every material possession. Was I grieving over the shame? No, *he* bore the shame for me. I loved *him* with all my heart. He gave me strength and courage to go on, hour after hour, day after day.

Long before I met James, or knew there was such a man, the still, small *voice* had spoken to me in the darkness and depths of an autumn night.

"You shall bring forth a *son*, and shall call his *name* Jesus."

Though to have a son would be the greatest of blessings to me, how could I have a son without a husband? I did not expect to have a husband but just to live for my Lord. My life belonged to *him* alone. But this man, James, was chosen and called to walk with me the path that carried me through *the valley of the shadow of death*. Psalm 23:4. Yes, and through death itself and hell. I could not escape the portion allotted to me, though in my ignorance of God's *way* and *will*, I strove with all my rebellious heart to do so.

When I had parted from my companions of a happier life, I had left even my personal belongings (except a few clothes in a little traveling case) because *he* had said,

"You must forsake all." Luke 14:33

Then I went to the poor and humble home of a childless couple who offered me a home, such as it was. After a few weeks James came to this same home and one day, kneeling before these two people, we said our vows as husband and wife, sincerely believing we were. We still believe that God joined us so, but we believed we should live, although together, separated from the marital relation.

At this time our kind friends provided us with food twice a day; before we went to walk and have meetings, and again on our return late in the evening. We ate with them, poor food but good enough for us.

After some weeks our friends moved into a smaller house and we had to find a place of our own where we could live. We succeeded in locating an empty shack into which we moved. Our friends supplied the meager rent, for it was so bare and so small a place, without any comforts. There wasn't even a stove to warm us or to cook our scanty food.

After a few nights James, on arising in the morning said, "Let us go and get a stove."

"Where can you get a stove?" I asked. For I knew he had nothing to buy anything with, and that no one had given us a stove.

"The Lord showed me a stove in a dream last night."

So we walked and though he did not know there was a city dumping ground there, having never been there, straight to the place we walked. There was the stove, old and battered, but whole! A pipe was there too, to fit the stove. It was light because it was sheet iron, so we had no difficulty carrying it home. How glad we were! But we were even more blessed in finding wood thrown away too at the same place we found the stove.

We had no coffee, no tea, no milk to drink, but we were content, and were being drawn nearer together day after day. At nights the hours were all spent in each others arms.

Several months later in the year, sitting on a high hill as we rested after walking miles, we read our Bibles until James wearied. He lay down on the ground, his Bible resting on his breast, while I still sat by his side reading.

"Will you read to me?" he asked.

I did so, reading in the *book* of the history of Abraham. Suddenly the words came to me of the *promise* made to him that his wife should bear a son in that set time next year.

"There will be a son born next year." I said wonderingly to James.

"It will never be my son! I would rather have my head cut off before I would ever do anything to bring a child into the world."

"Well, I would do nothing against the *will* of our precious Savior."

Will you notice this son *he* told me I should bear in the next year was not named? But the *promise* of that *son* given me two years before, I was told to call *his name* Jesus. I did not see the difference, for a spiritual *son* to a natural woman was beyond this woman's comprehension. I thought and believed it was a natural son, spoken of at different times.

Later that day, when we were in our home before going to have meeting, a strange thing came to me, like waves or strong winds—a desire that was overpowering in intensity, a thing I had not know before. James was standing on the other side of the room.

"Come and hold fast to me," he said.

This I did, putting my arms around his thin waist and grasping him tightly in my arms. At once that storm was stilled, leaving me as suddenly as it came, just as when a strong wind ceases.

The next day the same thing came to James. Strangely this did not come to us at nights when we were in each others' arms, nor when we walked together or sat near together, but when we would be separated by the few feet, the width of that small room in which we ate our food. This continued for days and grew harder to bear.

"Oh, dear God," I prayed, "don't let it come to both of us at once."

He answered that prayer, but in my agony of unbelief, of uncertainty, I separated myself from my companion for many days and nights, which for weeks we had spent together, close in each others' arms, as little children who love each other in innocency. I feared that if we should yield to that storm, we should be lost.

At the time of this separation, we walked together, read our Bibles, and prayed as usual. We went daily to the streets and sang the songs and preached *his* words.

After seventeen nights had passed and midnight had come, the sweet, still *voice* came to me.

"Arise, and go to thy husband."

I had thrown the precious Bible out of the room several times when James brought it to me to show me some words he had been given by the *spirit*. My Bible was not being used, only as we read together or preached together in those seventeen days. My heart was hardened, but that night I prayed God to forgive me. Then feeling *his* sweet pardon, I went to James's room. He gently took me into his arms and the miracle that caused our son to be born in the next year was accomplished.

The morning of the next day, following that midnight with dawn, was the fourth of August. Then I told James of God's confirmation of the conception.

"The child has been conceived, God has given me a sign."

I wonder how many mothers have longed for a son as I did? How many mothers have known in just a few hours a son was conceived? I knew it because God told me so, and so I told James. He did not receive the news with joy, but shook with sobs.

"I will have to suffer!" he cried.

Oh yes, but neither of us knew how terribly nor how long that suffering would be!

During that night of the fourth of August, when our son was conceived, no storm was within us, just a feeling far removed from lust or fleshly desires. You men and women of the world may not believe, but the *one* we shall serve until time shall be no more, knows it is true, and I know if you are given wholly to *him*, *he* can and will do the same for you. We were in a place where we knew we must depend on *his* words and *his spirit* for all our needs. Judge us if you will, condemn us, scorn us, hate us; we do not feel any of those things, for *he* is our *shield*; *he* is our *rock* in whom we live, for *he* is our *life*.

In those faraway days, three times *he* showed me an old fashioned quart cup with my eyes open, seen as through a cloud, and spoke these words to me:

"Will you drink this cup for *me, my* child?"

My reply was always:

"I will Lord, I will, I will."

But if I had known the threefold bitterness of that cup of death, which I had to drink to obtain *life*, I would have said,

"No, Lord, I will not drink it. I cannot drink it."

How many know what that cup of threefold bitterness is? Many, no doubt, think they do.

How many, many times in the days of darkness, the days when I had no understanding of the *scriptures*, I laid the Bible on my knees saying,

"Father, I cannot understand it. I'll leave it just as it is until *you* give me the understanding," for as I read there seemed to be contradictions in the words before me. But now and ever since *he* gave me understanding of the *scriptures*, I know and have known contradictions are not in the Bible, but in the minds of people without understanding of the Bible.

Often I heard men and women preach, giving what to their minds was meant by passages of *scripture*. But these explanations were just products of their own imaginations, or "vain traditions received from their fathers," as Jesus said. Their teachers were those who taught for money (collections or donations, salary, etc.,) after money had been paid by them or by someone else, to study under these "temples made with hands." It is written, "They ran but I never sent them."

You, some of you will say, "Who are you to attempt to teach us?"

Years before, with uplifted Bible held high, I had promised to go with *him* all the way. In the days of persecution a song *he* gave me often came in my mind.

> "Jesus, can the thorns be sharper
> Than composed *your* crown for me?
> Is the cup I drink more bitter
> Than *yours* in Gethsemane?"

That small, sweet *voice* often spoke to me with precious promises and comforting words, that sweet *voice* no human ear can hear, for it is not audible. The words of poems *he* had given me as:

> "Oh, can you not follow *me* through the Red Sea?
> Or do you it's dark waters dread?
> March on, faithless child, *he* will pilot you through,
> For Jesus is walking ahead."

Strange as it may seem, when I learned that August morning that a son should be born to me, I felt no sin, no shame. The thing God had purposed us for had begun. He had begun it and *he* would finish it, we knew not how. It was an inexorable fact that I should have a son, not born of human desire, not by our seeking. Who will believe us? It does not matter, nothing is too great a sacrifice for what I have gained. We have not told it to the world, but now it must be told.

All the principals in this drama of life are old like myself, or as I know, many of them have passed to their reward. No more can they reproach, no more cast a stone, nor could they if they wished, ask forgiveness for such needless cruelty and scorn.

"But the thorns were not too sharp, dear Savior, and the cup was not too bitter, for even in hell *you* made it bearable for both James and me."

At last I was thankful for everything, thanking God for *his* wonderful works to let me know the inside workings of evil without being partaker of the corruption, and also for having known the tortured souls who are without hope in hell. Judge us to be insane, judge us to be criminals as you choose, it will not ever hurt us. God gave us a work and we did it with *his* help and love. We have gone through the judgment of hell, but *he* was there—there with us through the hottest of the fire, as *he* was with the Hebrew children in the fiery furnace. We thank God for the privilege that we were given to suffer shame for *his name's* sake. Do not think it was easy, or that the fire was pleasant, but be glad that at this time somebody paid the price through Jesus to save you—yes, and all the world from the punishment, the untold horrors of hell.

One day, when James had gone to the large market to get some little foods, I began to peel a potato for our supper when I saw a clot of pure, dark blood on the potato. It was real blood, but I had felt no pain from a cut. I examined my hands thoroughly, there was no cut, no slightest abrasion. Then I examined the potato, it was a nice, smooth potato which I had washed before beginning to peel it as I always do with all fruits or vegetables. There was no worm hole in that potato, and I had never seen insects with blood in them unless it had been sucked from the veins of people or animals. The potato was perfect. Then I took a small, white piece of cloth to save that blood clot to show to James on his return.

I was a little afraid, it was so strange. For this reason I fell to my knees beside the hard, little slat bed and my soul cried out to God.

The first words of *his* answer were spoken to me.

"Without the shedding of blood there is no remission."

And then he said to me,

"You shall bring forth a *son* and shall call *his name* Jesus Christ."

The first time he told me of a son *he* said, "You shall call *his name Jesus*."

The second time *he* did not tell me any name, and this was the third time. His sweet *voice* was not to be mistaken by any other voice. I was not happy at this marvelous news, but I was humbled and almost afraid.

I met James outside the door and at once told him what had been spoken to me during his absence, and showed him the white cloth with the blood stain; for the clot had soaked into the cloth, a soft fabric. He marveled at the blood and I told him the *scripture*.

"The Lord also told me about our *son's name* as I walked home," he said.

We did not know that the *son he* had *named* was not our small son, but the *son* of God, which was never contained in the mortal womb of mothers or a mother. That *only begotten,* which is the *word*, that *son* is born through the *words* of Jesus in the mind of the *redeemed*, and was manifested through the mouth of Mary's son, and after by the *disciples* and *church*, which was murdered as was Jesus.

We did not know what that blood on the potato meant; we did know it was a *sign* from God. Now we know what it took long years of anguish to learn.

We did not give up our long walks to the hills, we still walked to the street, meaning to do *his will* with all our hearts. But always before us was the certainty that we would suffer for breaking the law. But we had no fear, had not the *spirit* done the work in us? Had not *he* taken two, who were willing to obey *him*, and work out *his will*? And were we not as "clay in the potter's hands?"

Will the world, for which the price was paid unconsciously by us, for the love of Jesus Christ and humanity, ever understand and cease to condemn? That is our *father's* business.

Four and one half months passed by from the time of our son's conception. Then the blow fell. Much more grievous than we could have thought ourselves worthy. Such punishment we could not have imagined, but we met it without protest, without murmur or complaint. For me it meant such physical agony as no human could have endured without the *power* of God to sustain me. It meant ostracism from my fellow beings. I might indeed have been a leper in the eyes of the world. Did it matter to me what the people thought of me? No.

People in the world cover their doings and think no one knows what evils they are hiding. We hid nothing. We earnestly and solemnly knew what we had done was what we must do, and we knew it was not of our choosing. Calmly we faced a future which contained we knew not what, for ourselves and our son, who was to be born. We had expected a jail sentence, or even a penitentiary term, but not what was meted out to us.

One day the dear *voice* said to me,

"There is a great work to be done, and no one can do it but you."

The fourth or fifth time I met James, we went to a mission one night to bear the *message* of God had given us—the great *message* of *his name*. A man sang a solo, over and over he sang,

"God will take care of you. He will take care of you."

He did not take his eyes from my face as he sang that song, and I knew God had it sung for me. *His promise* that *he* would take care of me, and through everything *he* did take care of me. This man did not know me, having never seen me before that night. All the people there were strangers to us both, but they could not understand the *message* so plain, because they believed in the teachings of the "blind leaders of the blind."

In those days when we preached on the streets, one young man asked me if I was to be the mother of Jesus? That was before my son was conceived.

I said, "No."

It was so strange that a stranger should put a question to me, who preached my *heavenly father's name* at the only place I could speak. People in missions pushed me out with their hands; they cursed me and said they would cast the devil out of me. I could smile in their faces, because I was happy and innocent, never expecting anything such as being the mother of a child to a man I scarcely knew, and knew nothing of his life before I met him.

Soon after that a man of perhaps forty-five years, a strong, handsome man, probably wealthy, came to the house to talk with James and me. He supposed, as did the others, that we were married by the law to each other, and on two occasions he asked us if we would confess that I was to bring forth the child Jesus. My child was not conceived at that time.

"No!" we both said.

"If you will confess this to me," he coaxed, "I will throw in everything I have into your work, because I believe you. Someone at this time must bring forth the child Jesus. I am a Roman Catholic, but I will cast in my lot with you."

"We cannot do that," we replied.

We never saw him again.

Days went on and yielding to *his will* in all things, as I understood *his will*, telling *him* to do with me as *he* chose. Ask yourselves if God had *revealed his name* to you, had told you as *he* told *his disciples*, if *he* had become the very joy and life in you, if you had forsaken all else for *his name's* sake, would you have said, "No Lord," after vowing to serve *him*? To obey him? Suppose you had been given the "first touch" but had not washed your blind eyes in the pool of Siloam, would you question God?

If you knew, as we knew, that millions of true men, women and children had perished from the earth in all manner of horrible deaths, because they loved and worshipped the God whose *name* they adored and whose words they obeyed, would you vow as James and I vowed (yes, as I vowed before I met James) that gladly we would follow Jesus knowing that death could not separate us from God?

For it is written, Romans 8:38-39, *"For I am persuaded that neither death, nor life, nor angels, nor principalities, nor powers, nor things present, nor things to come, nor height, nor depth, nor any other creature shall be able to separate us from the love of God, which is in Christ Jesus our Lord."*

The beautiful thirty-fifth verse of that chapter reads,

"Who shall separate us from the love of Christ? Shall tribulation, or distress, or persecution, or famine, or nakedness, or peril, or sword?"

James and I proved these most blessed words of the most precious *book*, while our God was proving us in the "furnace of affliction."

Would you, hearing that sweet, inaudible *voice*, sweeter than the voices of mother, father, husband, wife, child or sweetheart, that *living voice* which no earthly ear ever heard, deny *him*, *who* gives *life* freely to all who seek after *him* with all their heart? Then we did not know how to follow Jesus. We were blind, and blindly we followed *him* to death and hell.

When anyone asked us, we said that we were husband and wife, and we believed it. But the time was here that we must suffer for breaking the law of man, for living in what the world calls "sin," as we were compelled to live, that we might learn the deepest depths of hell and the highest heights of heaven.

After ages of darkness, how was one weak woman, un-skilled and unlearned, to find the *truth* of God which was hidden from the great and wise men and women of the world's religions? I did not find it, but God *revealed* it to me after I had suffered many years seeking for it.

Moses led the children of Israel in the wilderness for forty years, and John the Baptist came preaching in the wilderness of Judea. Was it anything to be marvelled at that one woman such as I could not find the *way* out of the wilderness? But God showed me the *way* and *he* gave me the *keys*. It is "*so plain that a wayfaring man, though a fool, need not err therein.*" Isaiah 35:8. It is so plain that a little child can understand it, can see it, and walk in it.

When I saw the thorns and iron spikes and walked over them, as I closed my tired eyes at night, I knew they were the persecutions of my daily life. That I could understand, but I could not understand the *scriptures*, taking them literally, having no *revelation* of them, only those pertaining to the *father's name*. Yet, it was to be many years before I understood fully the meaning of the great *name* of Jesus.

Thousands still believe that Jesus is coming down from the sky to take them up. I have heard preachers say that *he* would take them up above the earth and hold them there until this earth is destroyed and *he* had made a "new heaven and a new earth." Then *he* would return them on earth again. He will never come down out of the sky, nor will *he* ever take anyone up into the sky. Yes, *he* will catch up *his* own; but not up into the sky nor above the sky. He will catch them up into a full understanding, into *life eternal*. "He shall rule and reign on the earth." Not everyone who calls *him*, "Lord, Lord," will be caught up into that "*life* more abundant," but those who do *his will*.

I knew it was hell and the first night we were taken there, for my Lord said in that dear *voice* to me,

"This is hell."

I never doubted for an instant, but still I thought heaven was above the sky. But shaken was my belief, which had not been confirmed at that time, by my Lord. However, that heaven, man-made, was soon to pass away, and God's true heaven to be *revealed* to me, after I had suffered enough to know.

Here I must tell you that James and I were never guilty of teaching anyone to do as we had done, for we knew that we alone were appointed for that place. Husbands and wives dissatisfied with each other, unhappy and preparing to separate, we tried to reconcile to each other. We tried to save them worse things, greater unhappiness. Sometimes we succeeded in keeping them together. We told them the *name* of Jesus Christ reconciles and makes one. We told them to obey the law, keep the *commandments*, do not commit adultery, and always do not kill!

On the night of December 16, James dreamed of two barrels filled with leaves. Hidden under the leaves were two snakes, one in each barrel. We were standing outside when the snakes came out of the barrels and bit us. The blood streamed out of the bite on me a little way on the ground, but the larger snake that bit James, caused him to bleed profusely.

We knew afterward, that this signified the length of our imprisonment, his much longer than mine. At our breakfast in
the morning he told me the dream, and clearly it stays in my
mind for it was true.

They came later that morning of December 17th, two
plain clothes men; and we wondered why they had not taken
us when we were at street meetings, each day, openly before
all eyes.

I was in the kitchen when they knocked on the door.

Everyone was welcome in our humble abode. I met them
and asked them in, thinking they had come to hear God's
message. Their words dispelled the hope.

"Show us your bedroom. Who occupies this room
with you?"

I answered, "My husband."

"Come with us."

I was wearing one of the two gay, flowered kimonos I
had recently made, for I could not with comfort wear my
clothes, so I asked the men just one question.

"Will you let me change my clothes?"

"Yes."

They left me in the room, and I closed the door.

I had borrowed a long, full skirt and large blouse from
my only woman friend left to me, to wear to night meetings, putting my long coat over them. These things I put on.
I was not going to wear them at a wedding as "something
borrowed," and I had no pretty blue garter and no pretty
wedding gown. I did not know where I was going, or what
would befall me when I got there.

While I was changing into my borrowed finery, the men
had found James reading his Bible, which he loved more
than anything his eyes could see. They gave him the same
command they had given me.

"Come with us."

He packed his change of clothes, his handful of clothes, and I packed my gay kimonos and my few, very few, other clothes.

We were ready.

As James and I stepped out the door of our home, one of the plain clothes men barked once more.

"Walk in front of us."

So we preceded them to the streetcar. They did not offer to touch us then. On leaving the streetcar we saw we were at the jail. Going before them as they commanded, we walked up that steep, long flight of stairs, and a door was opened by an officer in uniform.

We entered a room in which there were a number of officers. The two men who had escorted us there faced us again.

"Sit down," they ordered.

Then the officer in charge began to question us. This, my first and last jail experience, lasted just a few hours. But this was the first lap on the way to hell.

No, I was not afraid, just resigned to whatever came, and I did not know what it was that was to come. All the preceding months had, unbeknownst to us, prepared us to suffer.

James was calmer than the men who had brought us there. I wondered what they would do with us, and they surely did what they could, for we were made an example for all the world to see. God does all things well. We feared only *his* displeasure. We had no fear of what the authorities could do to us there, or anywhere.

We answered all their questions truly. They asked us about many *scriptures*, seemed astonished that we knew so many so perfectly, said they never knew anyone like us. What they said or thought of us mattered little, for we were not our own. We had been bought with a *great price*, and we had a price to pay in return.

As I sat there, I wrote on a paper a few characters in the "shorthand" God had given me years before. The officer took the paper from me, then handed it back.

"Read it," he said.

"I cannot read it."

Then he handed it to James.

"Read it."

James wrote the interpretation:

"All the gods of the nations are idols, but our God made the heavens."

That was all. The officer said nothing, but we knew it was the answer of God for us.

Of the dinner at jail, the rotten beef that stank so it nauseated me, the bread without butter, the simulated coffee, the beans, the dry boiled potatoes, there is no need to elaborate. I did not partake of this food, as the odors are still vivid in my mind.

The language was such as I never heard from human lips, certainly not from animals. Blistering oaths, sewer, obscene, filthiness. I could not go away from it, for I was locked in with it. One, just a girl, and nearing the time of the birth of her baby, said she wanted beer and sang and danced. How horrible she looked with her swollen face and distorted body.

But what came afterwards was far worse.

James and I were "grilled" again after dinner. Then at about four-thirty, a strong armed, steel fingered woman, took me by one arm, one of the plain clothes men who brought us to the jail was grasping my other arm, and they dragged me down that long, steep flight of stairs from the jail.

"Oh, please let me walk," I begged. "I can walk."

I was afraid they would injure my son, my precious one they knew nothing of, and probably would have hated as they hated me.

Roughly I was pushed into a car. The guards took their places, one on each side of me, not letting go of my arms for a moment. I looked back to see if I could see James.

"Where is my husband?" I asked.

"He will follow in the next car."

I learned afterward that one of the men we first met at the house, and another tormentor, held James as they had held me, all the way to the next lap on the way to hell. We made no resistance, we made no complaint. There was no reason for their cruelty, but they wanted to hurt us. Were they qualified to "cast a stone" at us? I think not.

That afternoon, on arriving at the psychopathic ward of the old, malodorous hospital, I was taken into the first "padded cell" I had ever seen, and did not know then what it was called, for it was not "padded" with anything but hard, bare walls and floor. The strong armed woman let go of my aching, bruised arm, another woman made me undress. I did not refuse her order. She took my clothes, letting me keep my own gown, and put me into a tub.

"I have bathed today," I said, (in a clean tub).

"We give another bath."

She was not ungentle with me, and when the bath was over she left the cell, taking my clothes away with her, but leaving my precious Bible with me.

It was still light enough for me to see to read, so I read my Bible and prayed for James, wondering how he was. I had asked the woman who gave me the bath, "Where is my husband?"

"In the room above this," she had answered.

Soon someone unlocked the door, saying nothing, and brought a tray containing uninviting food and water. I did not touch it. Afterward another one came, unlocked the door, and again in silence took away the untouched tray.

I did not sleep all that long night. At short intervals a light was flashed in my face and I, having heard the noise of approaching footsteps, had kept my eyes closed feigning sleep. At last the night was gone.

The door was unlocked and a tray was brought in with some more ill looking food and some counterfeit coffee. I did not touch the tray. My clothing, including my borrowed clothes, was returned. I washed and dressed, combed my hair with my own comb for the last time for many long months, read my precious Bible for the last morning I would read it for many months, then I was led into the "court room" where people are supposed to be tried and proven innocent or guilty.

The court room had a number of spectators, the judge, officers and I suppose a few attaches of the law, but no jury. I was seated on entering the room, opposite the judge. He was a large, handsome man, with big, soft, kind-looking, dark eyes, and black, wavy hair. His hair was ornamented with a rather long lock which grew in front, a beautiful silvery lock, that looked like bright silver in his abundant hair. I had one such lock too, in the back of my hair, just above the right side of my neck. My hair was brown, curly and shot with red-gold, for the red grew among the brown. My eyes were blue, but one was flecked with brown.

The judge asked me just one question.

"Do you claim this man James to be your husband?"

I did not call him "your honor" when I gave my answer.

"Yes, I do. And *what God hath joined together, let not man put asunder!*" Mark 10:9.

He spoke one more word to me.

"Committed!"

To what? I did not know and did not ask then.

As I was being led out of the court room, I saw James being led into the room by another door opposite the one they had brought me in by, and were now taking me out of. When I saw him I held back, hoping to hear what was told him, and what he would answer the judge, but I was jerked forward, and taken back to the cell out of which I had gone a few minutes before.

In the cell I was confronted by the same two men, who took us from our home the morning before, and a witness not belonging to the law. There they presented me with the warrant, which was to have been served on me at the time of arrest, but was withheld until now. I read it in wonder, for it read like this, word for word:

This woman is violently and dangerously insane, and if given her liberty will destroy her own life or the lives of others."

It would have been laughable had it not been so far from a laughing matter. I had never in all my life harmed anyone, but had fed and clothed and sheltered in my home many poorer than I. But that home was gone forever. I had cared for mothers in childbed, had taken care of sick, sat up with man ill and sorrowing.

Harm anyone? Never!

Take my own life? Never!

For I knew my life was not my own, and to take it would be murder, as much as if I took the life of anyone else.

I confronted those two men as I read their lying affidavit.

"You have signed lies. You have perjured your souls before God. You will be judged by the *judgment* of God. You know we are not insane."

One man took off his hat, which he had not thought worth while to remove in my presence, and he also did not take it off at the mention of the *deity*; but he took it off to slam down on the table in front of him in anger, to emphasize his words.

"Damn your Bible! God is of no more virtue or help than my hat!"

He paused a moment, then went on.

"You do not have to go."

Still I did not know where, nor did I ask, "Go where?"

"You can go home. Give up this man, give up that Bible, and stay at home."

My arms went up high without any will of my own and words came out of my mouth.

"I will never give up what God has given me. I will rot in ____" (the name of the place to which they were going to take us) "before I'll give up what God has given me."

This name was not even a familiar name to me, and had never had any meaning. I had no room in my mind for such a place. If I had known what it meant, the words spoken blindly then would have been:

"I'll rot in **hell** before I'll give up what God has given me."

They took me out of the cell, that strong armed woman of steel materialized, taking one arm in a clutch that hurt. The man (who had blasphemed God's *holy name*, which I had told him) on my other side. Downstairs, James with his cruel guards awaited. Together we were then taken and ordered to get into a strong vehicle drawn by mules. Poor mules, they too were captives, but I know they could eat the food given them, for they were sleek.

I had been careful all this while not to let any of these people know about my unborn son, for I thought if they

knew they might not let me go with James. I knew that
James would not be in custody if he had not believed me
when I explained the *father's name* to him. I also knew that
he was innocent as I was, and was determined to share any
punishment meted out to him.

The man's offer to me that I could go home had not
temptation for me. Not even the kind-eyed Judge guessed
my secret, for it was not yet visible. Long after that fateful
day, I asked James about his experience in that psychopathic
ward. He told me that it was identical with what I told him
of my own experience. That he had spoken the same words
to the judge that I had spoken to him.

The man who drove the mules seemed to assume the
place of a questioner, or perhaps he thought our answers
would further condemn us in their sight. We met all his questions with calm answers of *scriptures*, for all the questions
he asked called for *scriptural* answers and God gave them to
us, as *he* had promised. He asked us of the *commandments*,
we repeated them, told him where they could be found.
At last the mules had taken us to the railroad station, and the
train with its barred car into which our captors led us, not
leaving us to walk alone.

The train was on its way. The strong armed woman was
my only guard on the locked and barred train, but a guard
sat on each side of James. Fearlessly he began to talk God's
words to them, just speaking the *words* of Jesus we both
loved so much.

"How well he talks," my guard commented.

In my ignorance of conditions in the place to which we
were being taken, I asked if we could preach there, for now
I knew where we were going for I had asked the officer who
drove the mules, and he told me.

The woman answered, "Oh, yes, I think they will," but she knew for a certainty they would not.

After a while James's guards grew angry and wanted to stop the flow of words, dear, pure words of Jesus, coming from his lips. How I loved to hear them and how long it was before I heard them again from his lips!

One of the men said to the other:

"We'll put him in hot water when we get him there."

James answered not one word; he bore all their insults in silence. For weeks that saying caused me anguish, for I could not know what they did to him there.

After several hours we were near the place of our punishment. The train came to a stop.

Standing at the station was our conveyance. We were not met by a welcoming band, no smile there, no friendly face. The poor old man who took us on the last lap of our journey to hell, spoke no word to anyone.

We rode in a slow, aged cart drawn by a large, old, raw-boned white horse, and driven by this silent old man who never smiled. Neither did he speak to any of the ones whom he took to that place, where for many there was no hope. His soul must have been saddened by the work allotted him, bringing to hell souls to be damned.

This man met the trains three times weekly and bore it's grist of humanity destined for hell. By ones, twos and up to six at a time, as they were engorged by the justice (?) of this psychopathic court.

This day there were two—two who would not be forgotten there, and who would never forget. Two who suffered intolerably and paid their debt to the inexorable law of men "unto the uttermost farthing."

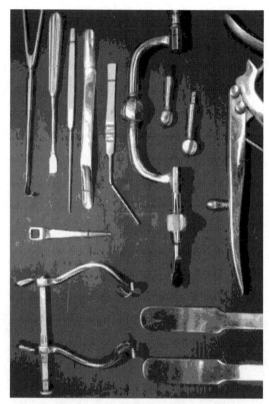

Some of the inmates were used as "guinea pigs" to test each new psychiatric theory, and procedure. The doctors routinely performed involuntary sterilizations on thousands of women and some men.

Part II
THE STABLE

IN THE HOUSE OF THE MAD

Have you ever been on the cattle range, where the herds
    are bedded at night?
Have you heard the thunder of summer storms, and seen
    the flashes of lightning bright?
Heard the restless roar of the wild herd, as they surge
    like the waves of the sea?
But the cow-boys surround and they can not pass, though
    they long and strive to be free.
The coyotes howl around the camp, longing to steal for
    their young,
And crickets sing in the grasses damp, while the cow-boys
    song is sung.

Have you ever been in the house for the mad? O, God!
Shut up for months behind iron bars, as you strove to
    follow the Christ
Who trod before, this way through hell?
All around you hear the curses, groans, the screams and signs,
    vile language, prayers, pleadings, heart-breaking moans —

Your "bed is made in hell, yet is *he* there."
Outside twittering birds in branches rest. Outside are
    God's blue sky and sweet, pure air.
As you lie in foul air with fast closed eyes, the sounds
    around you prevent your sleep,
You hear the many mingled cries of perishing sheep.
Sometimes from your aching heart comes the cry, "O, Lord,
    our gracious God, how long?
How wilt *thou* suffer this blight of sin, this living
    death, O, God, how long?"

Ah! Could you but choose, which would it be: to be
    herded in with mad creatures,
Who tear each one the other, as wild beasts tear
    lost humanity—
Or on the plain, in God's sweet free air?
Herder or herded, which would you be? Ah! The choosing
    is not for you, that is past.
As you bow to Almighty God, you say, "Not mine, but *thine*,
    O, Lord *thy will* be done!"
Though all unknown and dark the way, until in God's
    great mercy,
You shall see the *son*.

THE STABLE

The place was set at the foot of the mountains, and towering high above the others, one great mountain lookcd down silently, grimly, as if aware of the drama enacted before it's unmovable face. It's face was always watching but never joyful.

The sky was blue, and the sun was shining on a few fleecy white clouds, which looked like snow mountains or drifts of snow floating upside down on an ocean of pure and shining blue. Evergreens standing like sentinels, straight and proud with their young at their feet. Flowering Eucalypti, Magnolias with their sweet white blossoms, like those growing in many beautiful southern home grounds, orange, lemon and grapefruit groves, with their stately rows bearing both fruit and blossoms at the same time, like a mother who has born her first children so early that they have grown up and the babies of her later years are gurgling happily among them.

There were great pines, cedars and palms; and though it was December, the loveliness of their green foliage was comforting, for the trees are something God has given to all people to enjoy. It always grieves me to see a lovely thing like a green tree sacrificed to the axe.

The winter sun was casting its pale gleam over all the scene, enhancing its beauty, but on a nearer approach, the barred windows and strong iron doors also caught the sun's rays.

"Oh, what a beautiful place!" I exclaimed to the steel armed woman who had no mercy, no pity, whose life was hypocrisy and lies, trying by her cruel deeds to advance herself in the career of policewoman,

For the institution contained all kinds of beautiful trees, shrubbery, flowers, well cared for lawns, and wide, clean walks; it was so attractive with its tall, neat buildings, its clusters of cottages.

I had not seen the inside.

However, at first glance, the inside looked nice too, with it's wide, long halls, sleek oak floors (which I did not know I would help to make shine like that); but the bars were inside too.

I did not know it was hell until that night. A place of cruel torture, of starvation, of murder, of flagrant injustice, of hatred, of despair, of envy. For those reasons I learned soon that I had to suffer there.

There were great stone lions, one at each side of the entrance, as on guard. Their solemn faces, their colossal forms, man-made, a symbol of the power of the beast in men—evil power. They seemed to say, "There is no escape for you. We are on guard here."

But I took no thought of them, no thought of escape ever entered my mind there. I knew there was no escape for us but through our *father's name*; for this was my punishment for breaking the law of man. Though I might have cried, "My punishment is greater than I can bear," I did not. But many times I prayed God to let us die; to let them kill us after the little one was taken away.

I did not know that our death was not to be a physical death in that place, but death to all man's ways, "for *my* ways are not your ways, neither are your thoughts *my* thoughts, saith the Lord."

The woman held fast to my arm and James's guards held him fast until we were delivered to our present tormentors. We were completely delivered to them (they thought), but were under the protection of a *power* higher than they dreamed of.

This winter afternoon the mountain was looking down on another drama, a drama of life and death. Something unheard of before was taking place, as the old, rickety conveyance transported James and me to the end of that journey, which for many was truly the end of life. Afterward, seeing that conveyance working regularly, hot or cold, rain or shine, always bringing the loads of human grist, I named it the "Chariot."

The Receiving Cottage (or hospital) where James and I were taken, I called the "Old Grist Mill;" but the nurses both men and women, the attendants and even some of the people in bondage, called it "The Old Cow Barn."

In other words, "The Stable!"

It seemed that all the psychiatrists and nearly all the doctors were at the Receiving Cottage to examine James and me that late December afternoon, the 18th of the month. It might seem laughable to the people of the world that these learned and wise men and women gazed upon us as if we had descended from Mars, that we were beings of an unknown species. Then a tall, lovely, white-robed lady stood in the doorway, gazing, smiling as if we were highly amusing animals.

"How interesting," she said.

She could not know how very interesting it would be some distant day.

They had seated James and me in a large room as the officers had seated us in the barred car, one on each side, not near together.

"You shall never speak together again," we were told in that room, as we had been told in the barred train car. We did not answer.

"What is to be the length of our stay in this place?" I asked the white robed lady.

"Indefinite."

But we had a lovely and precious secret that we had not told; a wonderful secret that a *son* was to be born to us and through *his name, salvation* was to come to the world, so we believed. For we did not understand the *scriptures*. There was no room for *him* to born but in that dreadful place, mockingly called The Old Cow Barn. But I did not know how very soon I must disclose our secret, to save my son's life.

There were the psychiatrists, so wise in their own conceits—how could we blame them for scorning us? How could they understand a man and a woman who would step out of the beaten path of respectability to live together as husband and wife without sanction of the law? Doctors and scientists have never been able to find the soul of men or women; how could they judge us? We showed no signs of immorality, no signs of lack of intellect, no complaints for having been brought there. In fact we were calmer than they who so scornfully held us under the microscope of their minds as one would study some strange bug, while we sat quietly there before them that first day of our arrival in hell.

When the inspection had lasted long enough, James was taken away by two men. How I suffered for James, never seeing him, even at a distance during the many, weary, anxious days and weeks that followed. I went through those seven weeks of anxiety for him because I kept remembering the words of guards on the train, "We'll put him into hot water when we get there." (Long after that James told me that they had not done so.) But imagine if you can my gladness when, after seven weeks, I saw him walking in the sunshine, instead of being locked in a little cell, or tied to a bed as so many were, where I was incarcerated.

Here I will try to describe some of the keepers who tried in every way to shame us, to hurt us, who talked in our presence as though we could not see or hear. Who even said they had power to kill us — but they did not exercise that power on us, although I know many were murdered there. They told us that we should never see each other again, never speak together again; that we should never be free again. But they reckoned without God, whose we are and shall be forever.

The superintendent:

A man who was too handsome, with an effeminate beauty and perfection of face and figure, slender, broad-shouldered, proud. He was at least six feet in height, and had a winning smile when he wished to turn that smile on. It could also be a smile of derision and anger as he often looked at me.

Once he gave me a winning smile; that was the day he came back from vacation. He came to where we were sitting on the ground, after going around the circle as was the rule. He smilingly shook hands with our guards, then ignoring all the "patients," he came to me, smiling and extending his hand. I made no effort to extend my hand.

"Won't you shake hands with me?" he asked.

"I shake hands with my friends. You are my enemy. Why should you wish me to shake hands with you?"

He said not another word and walked away. In every way he proved himself my enemy. Was he now trying to blot out of my mind the hatred and disgust he had shown both James and me? I did not believe there was any change and after that, the events of more than two years proved that to be true. He was not changed toward us.

He had a wife and two young children living near by, and "patients" of the better sort were his "free" domestics. It occurred to me afterward, perhaps he was going to ask me to become one of his house servants. He knew that I was quick, clean and capable. Above all, he knew that I was not insane.

The tall, proud lady:

She looked enough like the superintendent to be his twin sister, but not related I was told. She walked as though her feet disdained the places they walked over. She was beautiful, and her dark eyes were beautiful when I saw them one day with a lady friend of hers who came to visit. Only that once I saw her eyes as a woman's eyes should look, soft and kind.

I did not know when I saw her the first day in hell, gazing at James and me so haughtily, so proudly, that I was to be her particular "allergy." She hated me intensely, but I gave her no cause. All the tasks she assigned me, I performed even as she would have desired. Never did I question her when asked to do anything; never did I ask a favor from her or any of the others. The cup was bitter, but it was given me to drink.

The red-haired woman doctor:

She was the visiting doctor, a red-haired woman in her early forties. She was short, stout and strong. A small, insignificant doctor, who knew less than she, was her colleague, taking the red-haired one's place when she was not available. He was a rat-like man, also around forty, ignorant, cruel.

Then there was a lovely lady called the **matron.** Both the matron and the tall, proud lady were in their thirties. There were two young girls, one *N. B., a graduate nurse,* the other *M. W.,* was in training. There was an *elderly graduate nurse,* a New England spinster.

There were two dear young women on night duty, who became my friends, and whom I loved. One of them was "an angel in hell."

There were many others, but these were the most familiar, because I saw them some every day, others very often.

James was led away by two guards and I by two women. They took me into a bathroom at the Receiving Cottage which looked clean. There they bathed me, not letting me bathe myself. Then they washed my hair in the same water and left it dripping, made no effort to dry it; and did not give me a towel. It was the night now, and cold.

Next I was put into a "padded" cell, into a bed which had a hard, hard mattress, one pillow fully as hard as the mattress, and sheets which were cold and clammy.

"Will you please let me dry my hair? I may take cold," I asked.

"No, you won't take cold," they said.

I did not know then that they did not care.

My Bible was my inseparable companion, but like everything else all my life, everything I loved was either taken from me by death or by circumstances over which I had no control. This first night of my arrival in hell my Bible was taken from me and I did not see it or have it in my possession again for months. When I saw my Bible, I took it without asking permission. After all I loved it and it was mine, but after one month it was taken from me again and I did not get it back until long months passed when I left that place forever.

My Bible has never been taken from me since. Now for many years I have not only loved it but have known what it means, because my Lord Jesus Christ made it alive in me forever. The *way* is plain before the eyes of all the world, but the *truth* and *life* of the *way* must be *revealed* by the *spirit* of *him* who sent it.

In a little while one of the two attendants brought a tray into the cell containing some coarse and uninviting food. She went out leaving me, after locking the door which they had also done at first. Coming back to take the tray, nothing was said, only I asked for a drink of water, which was brought to me in an old graniteware bowl.

I had not tasted the food, nor any food since the morning of the 17th of that month, when I had eaten a clean breakfast with James, and he had told me of his dream of the snakes. However, I did drink the water, but if I had known how those bowls were used, and where the bowl came from, I would not have touched even the outside of it. That was the last time for me to drink from a bowl from the so called "Water Section."

The young woman went out, locking the door, and no one entered the cell all night. All night as on the night before, I did not sleep, only closing my eyes when footsteps came near and a light was flashed in my face. They must have thought that I slept. I made no sound, no moan, although my tired and nauseated body could have moaned. There was noise enough without me adding to it.

First there came a great crackling and popping of radiator pipes (I did not know what the noise was then), then a great volume of screams, curses, loud groans, prayers, cries of "I want to go home!" A sound which even jungle beasts could not surpass. This was not one by one, but all united in one awful and blood curdling series of sounds, to which no one paid the slightest heed.

Then the sweet, still *voice* of my Lord spoke to me.

"This is hell!"

Not until then had I ever known what hell is. But it is hell, without controversy. No one, unless they have been "cast alive into the fire" as were James and myself, can know just what hell is, or the cruelty of it.

Morning came at last, bringing a woman who unlocked the door. The attendants all had a large bunch of keys which they carried on a chain around their waists. She gave me water in a basin and a cloth to wash my face and hands. Later I was to be introduced to the soap—yellow, vile, fish oil soap.

Another woman brought me a tray of food, then, because I feared injury to my son by the fast, I managed to eat some of that, to me, distasteful looking and smelling breakfast; drink that counterfeit coffee. When breakfast was finished, and after a little while two young nurses came, unlocked the door and entered the cell.

"We must get you ready for examination, for the doctor to see you," one said. When they came with their rigging and large vessel of strong soapy water, for bowel irrigation, I knew for my son's sake I could keep the secret no longer.

"Please use just clear water, for I am going to be a mother quite soon and you will hurt my little son." (Always I spoke of my son).

My condition did not show enough for them to notice and they would not believe me; not until the doctor made the examination.

After that viciously strong enema, I was sent into the small, bare, cement floored bathroom, where the pain was so bad that blood came from my tortured bowels, as I knelt on that hard, cold floor in weakness and pain, praying my precious *father*, Jesus Christ, would protect my little son. An hour of torture must have passed, I sitting on that cold iron bowl or kneeling in pain.

In the meantime the hard faced, red-haired doctor had come and was waiting for me. Her examination was rough.

"I will be a mother; please be careful for my son's sake."

She did not answer, and did not lessen her harshness.

"Well, I guess she was right about her condition," the doctor condescended.

That, my first fearful ordeal, was over; fearful for my child's sake.

Because I was calm and was not "disturbed" as the attendants called poor unfortunates whom they put into hot baths or hot packs, I was given a coarse, faded outfit of underwear and one of my gay kimonos to put on. I told them the skirt and blouse belonged to a friend from whom I had borrowed them—that I had promised her to send them back, when she bade me goodbye. They promised to send them to her, and I learned afterwards that they did.

Then I was promptly put to work, pushing a heavy block of wood with a large, long handle. This was covered with several thicknesses of old wool blankets. I learned my first day in hell that the long halls were polished four hours each day, two in the morning, two in the afternoon.

These floors were sleek and shiny, and caused the inmates to often fall on those hard oaken floors, but the people in charge did not care. The majority wore rubber soled shoes with wide heels, with the exception of the daintier ones who always wanted to look dressed up. These wore leather soled shoes with high, sharp heels, but never did they fall, to my knowledge.

Our day started at four-thirty each morning. I went through this same routine, with the exception of the first morning when I had to submit to examination. First, making beds, many others besides my own. These beds must look so neat on the outside, with the corners turned so nice and square. Next came dusting with a long handled mop under all the beds and in the hall. Then two hours of pushing the polishers, which was done by many women in the morning, until 6:30 when we went to breakfast.

Such a breakfast! *"Better is a dish of herbs where love is than a stalled ox with hate."* Proverbs 15:17. There was much hate in that place, but no stalled ox. No meat of any kind for us. But, before our incarceration, I had the "dish of herbs" with love, when James and I were together. Many days in the spring we had gone walking on the hills with our Bibles, where I usually read aloud to him. There we would gather the wild mustard which grew in such profusion. Many days mustard greens cooked in salt water was our only food, "with love"—the love of god for us and in us. To this day I long to go walking on the hills with my dear one, to gather mustard, and I wonder would it taste as good as then?

After breakfast I was taken to the basement at the Receiving Cottage and introduced to a tin tub with water and soap in it. A washboard was also given me to use, to wash out soiled dish towels. I tried to manage this work which I performed daily for three months, until no longer able to do this. Then I was given other work.

My first day in hell I learned much and suffered much, longing to see or hear from James, but to no avail. There were cleaning chores and work of all kinds going on all day. This was broken up by meal times which were: breakfast at 6:30 A.M., dinner at 11:30 A.M., and supper at 4:00 P.M. Each meal occupied fifteen minutes of time.

At 4:30 P.M., each day, we had to go to bed, and at night the madly insane, and bed patients made all the clean-up work for the following day.

At night there was hell turned loose.

Sometimes, almost every night people were given chloroform and smothered with hard pillows to silence them. I smelled that sickish chloroform so often. Only in such cases and under such conditions can anyone know what goes on in hell. It is hidden from all eyes and ears except the "things," the "cattle" appointed for the slaughter by every conceivable torture and evil device, and I was one of these so appointed, for they often told me so.

The horrors of hell, multiplied by all the hells all over the world. Human beings have lost all semblance to humans except caricatures of faces and forms; locked in padded cells at night, strait jackets, restrained hand and foot by being buckled to beds, *"Where the smoke of their torment ascended up forever and ever."* Revelation 14:11.

And what is the "smoke of their torment"?

Their screams of pain and fear, their cries for water, unanswered; their shrill laughter, their pleadings, cursings, prayers all going up in one great volume of sound, like the cries of wild beasts in the jungles. This was at night when people should sleep.

Darkness had come outside to join the darkness that was there day and night.

Hell is so beautifully camouflaged, on the outside, so beautifully garnished, swept and polished inside when officials are expected. Their visits are always known before they come. Oh, yes, but the opposite is the greatness, the graciousness, the sweetness, the *eternity* of joy which is heaven. There is a great gulf between and only one *way* to pass from hell to heaven. This I learned after I was released from hell.

To those who think hell is only an imaginary place of fire and brimstone, of devil's imps with pitchforks, of worms never dying, of smoke forever ascending up and souls forever crying out, "How long? Oh, Lord, how long?" I want to tell you that hell is real, just as real as the road you walked on to school day after day and year after year. Just as real as the warm fire you sat before night after night, when your day's work was done.

The fire and brimstone of hell is real, every word of that description is real, but not as men understand it. You cannot see that fire and brimstone, but you feel its heat and how very, very hot it is! The worm is the—but no, I will not tell you for you would not understand. Suffice it to say, it is after the same manner as the fire and brimstone, only in the opposite direction concerning the prisoners. The devil's imps with the pitchforks are very, very real and ready to prod the weak and ill and pitch them into the fire. Truly that fire is not quenched.

In Proverbs 26:20 it says, "*Where there is no wood, the fire goeth out.*" But wood is supplied every time the chariot comes with it's load. The fire is replenished from all over the earth.

In a few days I learned about walking "around the circle." The inmates who were able to walk were taken out by two attendants, one walking ahead the other at the foot of the line. Of course those who worked in the many industries (without pay) were never taken on those walks, and those who were locked in padded cells, or were bed patients, never went. This walk occupied about fifteen minutes, five minutes each way around the circle, five minutes to sit on the ground.

There were no chairs in the Receiving Cottage to sit on; no long benches ornamented the halls, so the only time we had to sit down was fifteen minutes at mealtimes, and the five minutes outside. Often in winter we could not go out because of snow or rain. My body was so fatigued, I began in the later weeks of pregnancy to crawl under the bed I occupied at night (I had a bed to sleep on at that time), but was always told to get up if one of the attendants came in.

At night before my little son was born, I met the sweet angel of hell, "Little Mercy." She let me get out of bed and sit with her in the hall, while Marie, another attendant, was at her midnight supper. Mercy sat, when her work was done, until she had to go the rounds again, and worked on garments for her little two and one half year old son. Her son was cared for by her mother and safe while she and her father worked.

We talked of the Lord always, for Mercy loved *him* in the only way she knew. She knew the *scriptures* too, and believed all that I told her. Her old grandfather was a Baptist minister she said, and she loved him dearly I know, as she so often talked of him.

Days and nights went on slow, slow feet. I was assigned by the proud lady to wait on the operative patients, to wash faces and hands, comb hair, apply ice cloths to fever-hot brows, give ice water to them to drink, and put hot water bottles to numbed feet, for they could not help themselves.

The terrible things I witnessed day after day, hurt for the sufferings of others, but I knew for the sake of my unborn son I must be calm at all times. I was grieving so much over the destruction of young womanhood, seeing young, beautiful women taken away to be operated, not knowing what was going to be done to them. No one was ever told. They were taken away, well and strong, but brought back in a few hours, some of them, some never again, moaning, soon delirious with fever. Oh, the pity of this destruction of bodies created for the glory of motherhood!

The two trustees:

One confessed to falsely witnessing that a young man had seduced her and caused him to be sent to prison for five years. I heard her tell this, and she was not under age, but in her twenties—a fallen girl.

Her very good friend was a woman in her thirties. Poor things! They were so trusted, so well treated! How could they ever guess they would meet the same fate as the many, many young girls they led away, ignorant that they were going to be slaughtered from their hope of motherhood. Some never to awake from the sleep of drugs. Some to awake, moaning, retching, burning with fever.

I was sent to care for them, bearing my unborn son, and grieving so for them. There were so many. Sometimes as many as six in one day to that ward. How many on the other wards, I do not know. It may have been that all the operating was done at the Receiving Cottage At the time, I did not know why I was privileged to see so much, although I never saw an operation, and would not have witnessed on if I could have escaped it. But I saw the effects of these horrors. The elder of the two trustees was crippled for life after her operation.

Often I saw M.W., the young trainee, coming out of the operating room with her white uniform much stained with bright crimson, with arms filled with sheets blood-steeped. I so frequently saw her scrubbing her hands and arms for the operating room, and then afterward scrubbing the floor and everything in that room. She was the only "nurse" I saw working, the others put the work on the slaves (patients).

Many were sent to hell to die, and their coffins sent on the train with them and stored in the basement until their bodies were placed in them to be shipped away. One who saw the coffins and that knew it to be true, told of a man sent to the basement one day and seeing a coffin with his own name on it, fainted away.

The Jane and John Does were not provided with coffins. I saw some bodies of women who died, taken by the nurses and jokingly sewed up in sheets. Men then took them and buried them in holes dug in the orchards, where the bodies would soon decay. How cruel, how horrible, I thought that was, to do to a human body! But years and wisdom have taught me the body is only the house in which the departed one used to live and moved out as we move from one dwelling to another, and, *"God giveth it a body as it hath pleased him, and to every seed his own body"*. 1 Corinthians 15:38.

(It does not matter what is done with my body, my dear, but if I could have it so there would be no flowers, no tears, but rather rejoicing, for I should have attained my reward according to the mercy of a great, just and merciful Savior.)

The bedding was the same winter and summer. That winter was extremely cold, and the summer following was extremely hot, but always those locked and barred halls and rooms, into which the sun never shone, were filled with fetid air.

One day each week beds were "aired" in this way: first the two sheets and one blanket were folded up, the mattress was folded over, which seemed an impossible feat because they were so stiff and hard. Next the sheets and blanket were placed on top of the mattress.

Once a year the mattresses were thrown from the second floor (or third floor as it might be) to the ground and covers and pillows thrown after them. They were all alike so we could never tell when those beds were made, whether we had the same ones we had slept in the year before. They were all evil smelling beds, because they had covered bodies of dead and dying, and never washed before they were used for someone else.

How my flesh cringed from those evil smelling bed clothes, so I always pushed the covers away from my face as I thought of my own sweet, sundried, clean beds where my home used to be.

Think, as you make up your beds with snowy white sheets, dried in life-giving sunshine, sheets soft and fine to touch. You sing with the birds in freedom and gladness, realizing your wonderful privilege of freedom—or do you realize? Perhaps not even thinking of that freedom; it is just your natural inheritance, just a matter of course. As the birds sing, do they take this freedom as a matter of course? Some do not, for they have escaped from captivity, or have seen their families taken captive and slaughtered by their enemies. They are praising God and singing of new nests hidden from the eyes of prying enemies, where their precious ones will one day sing, open wide hungry mouths to be fed by parents' care and God's bounty.

Think, you happy women, young or old! Think of thousands of women, young or old, behind iron bars, making beds each morning with gray, clammy sheets. Sheets that stick together because they are so damp, so clammy, so cold. The mattresses so hard, so impossible for you to imagine. Pillows made of the same construction, hard, cold or hot according to the season; but the sheets are always clammy and stick together.

You in your pretty colorful dresses and dainty aprons, would shrink from sight of these women. Why? These women are wearing old, faded, coarse dresses, all of the same pattern. Under poor coarse garments they wear scars, scars which change them from any hope of motherhood, of the clasp of baby hands, the smiles of dimpled faces, the sound of baby laughter.

Oh, you women who would destroy such innocence before it could nestle in your arms! Destroying also your own bodies, blackening your own consciences with torturing memories. You have sinned against God and the law of man; yet you believe it is hidden from all eyes, hidden in your tortured hearts!

How many of these women are behind those bars because they "took a way out?" How closely is the seat of life connected with your mind? Oh, mothers-to-be, thank God for the wonder, the joy He had granted you, and cherish that tiny seed of *life*. Do not cheat the world of one who may be intended to bless the lives of millions.

Remember, mothers who love your darlings, Romans 12:19, "*Vengeance belongeth unto me; I will repay, saith the Lord.*" You may see a still little form taken from your arms to be placed in a casket and lowered into the cold earth. There is no escape for you, but through sincere repentance, calling on the "*name* of the Lord" for pardon.

"*Though your sins be scarlet, I will make them like snow. Though they be crimson, I will make them as wool.*" Psalm 103:3. "*I am the Lord thy God, which healeth all thy diseases, which forgiveth all thine iniquities.*" Isaiah 1:18.

How blessed to keep in the *way* of *life*, so there will be no need for repentance. So that forgiveness will not be required of God for your sins.

THE SINNER AND THE SAVIOUR

"Come unto *me*, the Saviour saith,
Oh hear *his* voice today.
Why will you follow the paths of sin,
Farther and further away?

"Come unto *me*," *he* calleth again,
"Oh bring thy burden to *me*,
The heavy load by satan made,
Oh, come and thou shalt be free."

Freedom for me? Can it be that I hear?
Freedom, Oh glorious thought!
Bound hand and foot these many years,
I have served the devil for naught.

Hunger and thirst and aching heart,
And rags my portion here,
No *light* to shine upon my way,
Lost in the night so drear.

Thy *father's house* awaiteth thee,
The door is open wide,
The *name* on that door is plain to all,
'Tis Jesus the crucified.

The feast is spread for thy hungry soul,
He all thy need will supply,
And righteousness' robes for thy filthy rags,
That thou in *his* presence mayest stand.

"Lo! Here these two keys which I give to thee,
And priceless the treasures they hold,
Believe and obey the keys which ope' wide
The gate to the city of gold.

Lord, at *thy* hand these keys I take,
Plain is the *way thou* has made,
I'll take *thy* gift so freely given,
I'll believe *thy word* today.

These women behind the iron bars, made into beasts of burden, had close cropped hair and faces from which all hope has fled. Livid, scarred faces; faces that have forgotten how to smile. Faces upon which the tears had ceased to fall. Gaunt, undernourished frames, waiting only for the release of death.

What did they do to bring them to this place, which for them has no returning?

"I want to go home!" they cried day and night.

God is the judge of all men, but we who shirk the duty *he* has laid upon us, are guilty if we speak not to warn the people of *his* judgments; to tell them of *his* peace and pardon for sins.

Jane Doe:

One day a black woman was brought to the Receiving Cottage and she worked that day, not knowing what was to befall her. She was very quiet, very thin, almost emaciated. When the next morning came she was prepared to be operated on, but she didn't live through it. The elderly, graduate nurse, a very staid and pure maiden lady, who always watched over critical operative patients until they were better or died, came out of the cell into which the unconscious body was carried. When the body was taken away she sealed the room for fumigation. The day before, that poor, sad, lonely "Jane Doe" (they called her that) had worked so hard carrying dishes, setting tables, and doing many other tasks perfectly well and apparently healthy.

Ila:

The chariot brought Ila to the Receiving Cottage one cold December morning and I was sent to wash her face and hands before breakfast, and to comb her hair. She could do nothing for herself because her slashed wrists were securely tied. She had tried to take her life, but failing in the attempt she was sent to a place far worse than death in her home.

She was so tiny, so dainty, with grey eyes and soft, fine brown hair—a light brown. (She did not know that her hair would be jerked out by the roots by angry women who were supposed to help her get well.) She weighed ninety pounds and wore a number one shoe. Ila showed by her manner that she had been brought up in a highly elegant manner, educated and lovely, a partaker of all the good and costly things of life; and sheltered from the ills and rough things. How she came to be there, why she tried to take her life, I do not know; but even pretty dainty Ila may have been disappointed in love.

"Oh, this is heaven!" she cried out, as I went toward her to wait on her that morning.

"No," I answered, "this is hell."

When all her lovely, dainty clothing, all her personal belongings, all her costly cosmetics were kept from her, and horrible cruelties practiced on her helpless body, when her hair was being combed with a coarse comb used for many other heads, when she was made to disrobe completely and stand with "the cattle" as they called all of us, then she confessed, "This is hell!"

We all worked hard, but Ila would do nothing, not even make her bed. Excuses could be made for those poor, lost ones who had lost their minds, who knew nothing but of animal nature and then not even the nature of a clean, good animal. Nothing mattered to Ila but herself. Robbed of all her luxuries, her body clothed in abominable garments that looked so out of place on her, hair pulled out by cruel attendants to get her hands free of themselves, she began to know she was in hell, not heaven.

She discovered there was nothing heavenly about the angels who tore her hair out by handfuls, who roughly bound her like a mummy, but in hot sheets and blankets, trussed up so tightly she could move no part of her body, but only her head from side to side (she was not insane ever); then taking her by head and feet, two of them after wheeling her from the place where the hot water was, they literally threw her onto the hard mattress of the iron bed, no sort of pillow for her head.

Hot packs were supposed to be beneficial; but for nearly all I saw there, they were for cruel punishment. Ila was given no water of any kind (they were supposed to have ice water); there was no ice cold water left on her brow. I waited on many of the sick there, and they were given ice water to drink and ice cloths for their poor heads.

"How did you happen to see and know so much?" you might ask.

Well, one reason was that the authorities thought and often told me, that I would never get out of there. Another reason, was that though they called me insane, they knew I was not, but a quick, intelligent, good slave, knowing their every thought. Always ready to do all in my power to help the suffering ones. They did not ask me to assist them in horror of putting people in packs, and I would have refused to do so. Possibly it was because I told the red-haired doctor, "As long as your rules do not conflict with God's *rules*, I will obey them. But when they do, I will obey God," I said.

The expectant mother:

A girl was brought in one day, not very young, not pretty, and with child, at least seven months. She told me she had been a domestic in the home of a prominent judge in the city. This judge had betrayed her and sent her to that place to keep her silent. She was operated on, and a few days after that criminal abortion she left a trail of blood, as she pushed the heavy polisher hour after hour. If she survived, she could never be a mother. I never forgot the name of that aristocratic judge nor the fact that he had a young daughter, an attendant in hell. I do not believe the daughter ever knew this girl or knew her story. The girl chose to confide in me. I asked her no questions as we both pushed the polishers; I carrying my son, she robbed of hers. I have not told her story until now, and it should be told.

Yarba:

Yarba was a middle aged woman, dark and small, with no spare flesh, gaunt and scarred. I never heard Yarba laugh—I never saw her smile. Yarba was the only name I ever heard for her. I don't know where she worked in the daytime, but used to see her come in with the outside workers. All night I heard calls for her. How I pitied her, for it seemed that she could not get thinner.

"Yarba! Yarba!" they would call and she would get up and go without a word of protest.

She was doing the work that the attendants were paid to do; but the slaves did the work and received no pay. Yarba carried buckets of water—buckets of water too large and too heavy, mops and bundles of soiled bed clothing. The women attendants stood by and watched but did not work, only when wounds needed dressing, or some particular thing that needed doing and they knew that they would be found out if they neglected to do it. The slaves carried away the soiled things, mopping up the floors, but they of course were not permitted to handle implements of surgery.

My bed was next to Yarba's, so I heard her many summons. I lay quietly, not closing my eyes, until morning came at last at 4:30 A.M., with beds to make, others besides my own, floor polishing, dusting with the long handled mop and at six-thirty the call to breakfast with its fifteen minutes to rest. The attendants did not let poor Yarba nor me sleep in the daytime to make up for what was lost at night.

It is written *"They shall seek death and death shall flee away."* Revelation 9.6.

A young woman:

A young mother of seven little children was brought in one day and placed in a bathtub of hot water with a canvas cover exposing only her head. This cover fitted closely around the neck of the person in the bath.

This water therapy was supposed to be very beneficial.

Late that night I heard the attendants on duty talking about the young woman being dead in the tub when they found her. They had forgotten her and failed to give her the prescribed treatment of ice water to drink and ice cold cloths on her head. With the door closed, perhaps no one heard her cries for help. I do not know what was told to her family, and surely they must have been much grieved, for seven little children were orphaned of their mother, (as my brothers, sisters and myself, all small children, were left when my precious mother died).

Little George:

Little George was born in March but I did not see him until sometime in April, then a listless baby, not bright. His mother was a silly young woman of low I.Q. but harmless. One day the attendants took little George away from the ward and kept him away for hours. The mother nursed her baby and grew anxious at his long absence.

"When will they bring little George back?" she kept asking me.

"I don't know," was the only thing I could say.

When the attendants did finally bring little George back, he was very ill, drawn up as if in pain. I have always wondered what they did to little George during his absence.

Very soon after that, George's mother went home with him. She was very excited about going home, but being of a dull mind, realized little except that she was going. She loved her baby much—as much as she knew. Before I ever saw her she was operated, thus George would be her last baby. I wondered if she knew or cared. Poor little weak George!

The dressmaker:

She was a dressmaker from a city further south. She had much property, so she had been put in this place and kept there for years. The woman's son had done this dastardly thing, and death released her not long after my release from hell. She was an educated, refined woman much older than I. And she was my friend, which the proud lady did not know. During the five months I spent in that part of hell, she remained calm, quiet and helpful. She did beautiful work and helped me with some of my son's clothes before he was born.

The dressmaker worked, of course, in the sewing room, but one day she walked around the circle with the rest of us. As we walked, I saw her stoop and pick up something from the ground. It was a small piece of a carrot!

"You may have it," she generously offered.

"No," I answered, "eat it yourself."

Then she broke it in half, giving me half of it and keeping the other half herself. It was so small, just about two bites for each of us. We had not water to wash it, but rubbed it clean.

Oh, how good it was!

This was the only raw vegetable I tasted in all the long months in hell. Never any fruit! This dear lady, although she owned much, was not permitted to have her Bible nor was she ever given a newspaper or a magazine to read (neither was I). She loved her Bible and it would have been a comfort to her. She showed me the scars on her arms and legs made by cruel torture, and told me how she had suffered in hot packs—a diabolical punishment. I admired and pitied that fine, unselfish woman.

The pitiful girl:

She was a young and beautiful girl, with dark eyes and hair. She was kind and sweet to everyone; she worked faithfully and never complained. On a Sunday letter writing day, which occurred at two week intervals, she wrote to her parents. Before the letters were gathered up she asked me to read her letter. This is what she wrote:

"Dear Mother and Father, please come and take me home. If you don't I will not be here. Please come and take me home next Sunday, for I can't stand it here any longer."

There were no complaints against anyone; no words against their treatment of her, just a pitiful, girlish letter pleading her loneliness and need of her loved ones. But her parents did not come for her nor did they write, for all letters were brought into the ward.

However, before the second Sunday came, the coroner came to examine her dead body.

How did the proud lady explain that great lump on her head, just behind the ear?

Or how could she explain those terrible bruises on that white, slender body?

Perhaps that pitiful little letter was not sent to that grief-stricken family?

Yes, they came and took her body home! She never showed the least sign of insanity. How I grieved for that dear young life, so quickly, so cruelly taken away!

The Austrian woman:

The Austrian woman must have been in hell for some secret reason, for she was intelligent and educated, a hard working slave. She was a writer, but I never saw any of her writings. When we were taken around the circle, she used to gather Eucalyptus leaves to make a tonic for her hair. This was long and abundant without one grey hair, although she must have been in her sixties—at least I thought so, for her face showed signs of age. She had a slim, strong body.

One bed-airing day, the attendants took her writings from under her mattress when she was not in the room. She blamed me for not saving them for her, but I didn't know they would not return them to her, for at that time I was too new there to know their underhanded ways.

Afterward this poor woman tried to escape, but was brought back and punished. Later she did escape by getting to the reservoir and drowning herself, so I was told. That is all I know—anyway she was dead.

Miss Kelly:

Miss Kelly spent her nights as soon as supper was over, at 4:30 P.M., tied to her bed in a padded cell. And more, poor Miss Kelly was in a strait jacket every night for she was always "disturbed" when darkness came. Many nights I heard that bed shake as if it would be shaken to pieces; and heard a voice, never ceasing, a voice that sounded like an old-fashioned phonograph with a tinny sound. Then I learned it was Miss Kelly, who worked so hard all day, Miss Kelly who emptied all the food she could steal onto her plate, but who could blame her, she was thin, and she was starving.

One day I reached to get a potato and Miss Kelly, who sat beside me, attacked me, tearing my kimono from my shoulders. She could not harm my darling, then unborn; God kept him. But I did not get any dinner. It didn't matter to me. Once my friends sent me some candy which I miraculously was allowed to keep. Giving it all but one piece to Miss Kelly, she became my very good friend, as such a friend knew how to be. It is a wonder that I ever saw that candy! How glad I as to be able to help poor Miss Kelly to a little food.

While polishing the halls one day, I saw a small, emaciated woman fall under her burden of pushing a polisher. Immediately an insane person, holding a polisher, rushed at her, pushed the little sufferer and the polisher she had been trying to use off to one side of the hall, going on her fiendish way. After awhile the little sufferer was taken away by two attendants. I had not seen her until that day and never saw her again.

I saw people brought to the Old Grist Mill by the chariot that delivered them, brought there seemingly sane, well dressed, lovely young women; and in a few days they would be raving under the conditions there, put into hot packs, hot baths and tied to beds.

The blonde girl:

One day a little blonde girl of school age was brought to the "Cow Barn" as the women and men attendants called the Receiving Cottage, by her father. Did he believe that he was doing the right thing? She laughed at everything, because she was young and gay. How could she know what would meet her there? Perhaps death did. She was taken into the "clothes room" to be stripped of her pretty, fashionable clothing, by the proud lady, who took charge of her as her father left.

This child did not know that she would be dressed in coarse, faded rags. She must have rebelled, for when the woman brought her out of the sound-proof room, her little slender throat was peeled by cruel choking, almost to the bleeding stage. Tears were on her pretty face — tears of fear and bewilderment.

How could that stately, beautiful lady, who talked to her father in honeyed words, be so cruel? What a change in her deportment!

I never saw that little girl again; she must have been locked in a padded cell and tied fast to a bed. When I was sent away from the Receiving Cottage to the lowest hell, I looked for that little girl but she was not there.

The minister's daughter:

Another child was brought by her father. This one was, he said, thirteen years of age. But what a contrast to that beautiful, strong little girl who was choked. This child had the actions of a snake. Her body was snake-like; she crept on her stomach and they could not tie her fast enough to keep her in bed. I was to feed her, but she could not, or would not, eat.

Four sheets were used to tie her to the bed, but she squirmed out just as a snake would. Her father was a minister of a denominational church.

What awful sin had he committed? Perhaps on another man's daughter or son, that such punishment should come on his child?

This girl did not suffer, for she had no mind, just was a "poor little sawdust doll" — never speaking, perhaps not hearing, asleep in her poor little mind. The proud lady did not know how to cope with this case. She was afraid to destroy the child, so the next day after bringing her there, the father was sent for to take her away.

Sad? Yes. But not as sad as for others who could feel the horror of hell.

A young wife and mother:

Her husband came to take her home, and they had just passed outside the grounds when she was stricken by an epileptic attack. The husband, who had been so joyous a few moments before, drove back into hell broken-hearted. Epileptics were not released, so I do not know if this young wife was ever let out again. She was such a nice, friendly woman; with several children at home.

Lily W.:

Lily was a young mother who was taken away from her home and two children, one and two years old.

"I was washing clothes outside, when the authorities came. They made me go with them at once, and I have never heard since then, what became of my babies left playing in the yard," she sorrowfully told me.

A beautiful Mexican lady:

With the small, bent point on a treasured straight pin, this Mexican lady made lovely lace from muslin ravelings she collected from the sewing room, where she worked. She gave ma a gift of a tiny crocheted basket, but later that same day some one must have told the attendants, for the pin and the ravelings were taken from her. This dear, intelligent and beautiful woman could not have so much as a small pin to help her bear the endless drudgery and horror of hell.

The first hair washing day I experienced there, this lady was told to lean her head down in the tub, and one I had not thought cruel before, poured hot water on her head.

"Oh, the water is too hot!" the Mexican lady cried out.

But still the scalding water was poured over her lovely, naturally curly hair. Soon after that she was almost bald.

About two months before my son was born, the proud lady confronted me.

"What are you going to do about your baby's clothes?" she asked. "We don't provide free clothing for babies."

"I will write my friends, and ask them if they will send material, so that I can make my baby's clothes," I answered.

So, I wrote asking for enough white outing flannel to make skirts, bands, wrappers and three dozen diapers. I also asked for three long sleeved shirts, booties, several blankets, powder and olive oil. That was all.

After the things came the proud lady would lock me in a small, and at the time unused parlor room, after I had done the work allotted me each day. That always came first.

There I sewed and cried for my wee darling, and prayed. The proud lady gave me scissors to use while in the room, taking them from me when I left. Thread and buttons were sent with the material for his little clothes. You may know that I did not make these things with the joy most expectant mothers have as they sew so happily for their little ones, for I knew not what was to be.

This is the happiest time I experienced in hell.

Shut away from the hideous, unclean creatures for whom I felt so much sorrow. Shut away in a clean room, it was so quiet and restful.

At times as I was finishing the garments, I was allowed to take them out of the room with me, when the proud lady came for me. No need for scissors then, but she strangely let me use the needle. Then, that dear, calm dressmaker helped do some work on the little clothes for me. At last they were finished, taken away, and I did not see them until they were used on my sweet baby. I was too ill to wash them first, even if they would have let me have that pleasure.

One day as I was pushing a polisher, far too heavy for me, an insane woman pushed her polisher under my feet, throwing me heavily to the hardwood floor. I prayed that my little one would not be injured.

Another morning, having finished the polishing, I, with the others, were waiting the call to breakfast. An elderly and fat Mexican woman, also a polisher and slave, came up to me.

"I *named* a *name* on you were standing there," she said. "I called you Mary, the *mother* of God. But if you were, you would get us out of here, wouldn't you?"

"No!" No one but Jesus Christ can get us out of here." I answered

This Mexican woman was put here for the alcoholic cure. She was always kind to me, and I'm sure she would have been with me when my son was born, if she could have, because she loved me and I loved her.

While pushing a polisher on another occasion, I passed a bathroom with an open door, something I had not seen before. Those bathroom doors were always locked. This one contained an occupant in the tub of hot water. I did not recognize her, for only her head was visible, and her head was almost bald all over. I didn't know why then, that knowledge came later when I saw a young nurse tear her hair out. I had frequently carried dressings for the nurse some weeks before, and knew she had been operated and on her long scar had two tubes in it, to carry away the pus from her wound.

As I passed the doorway she was reciting meaningless words, as a child who has not yet learned to form words.

"Goop, boop, hiki boo," and many other sounds in a monotone repeated over and over.

Many days I passed the door, pushing the polisher and she began to call me, some days to curse me, as she intermingled her "bippy doo, chuckaloo, gookyskook." Other days she would say, "Come over my threshold, sweet Jesus," and smile at me.

Then one morning I was sent to give her ice water to drink and to put ice cloths on her hot forehead. Finally, I recognized her as one of those to whom I had previously carried bandages and other things necessary for her wound.

She was very ill, burning with delirium. It seemed she must die, but here she was for me to minister to. How long she had been in this place called the Receiving Cottage, I never knew. She was already here, so ill, when I was sent to that place which the attendants and nurses mockingly called the Old Cow Barn. We were called cattle and treated worse, for cattle are considered valuable and we were not.

So I was appointed Maud's caretaker, for I learned her name was Maud. She had no lucid moments; her life was all a blank. She too, would have died in that tub, as so many did, if she had not been cared for. I grew to love her, poor child, so she seemed. She shook the ice cloths off as fast as I could put them on, so I devised a way to tie them on.

Once while doing this, Maud spat in my face and laughed with glee, like a mischievous child. I went into the Water Section and washed my face at the faucet with cold water. There was nothing else, not even the fish oil soap. But that was the only time she spit on me, although she tried other times, but I was watching.

Her arms were fast, she could shake her head from side to side, but her feet were free. How she kicked that water, so furiously that the floor had to be mopped repeatedly. When I held the basin of ice water to her mouth she tried to knock it out of my hand with her chin. Sometimes she hurt my hands, but I was always tender with her. I knew that she had to have that cold water, but she did not, and I always persisted until she got all she needed, as often as she needed it. The tied napkins were renewed often.

So the days went by. It was polishers in the morning after bed making and dusting, in the afternoons caring for Maud. One day I was to her "Sweet Jesus," the next I was to her "the devil" and she cursed me. My love for her increased day by day, for she was a pitiful, helpless child. When Maud reviled me and yelled "I'll kill you!" I knew it was not Maud, but an obsession of evil power over her.

Before my little son was born, Maud was sent to the first lowest hell and I saw her no more until my baby was one week old, when she was brought back to the Receiving Cottage for a treatment.

There were some of these people in hell who had normal days. Often I comforted those who came to me for comfort, kneeling (which I never asked them to do) at my knees, asking me to pray for them. Unceasingly I prayed for them and for James and our unborn son. For myself I prayed, "Father, give me strength to bring *your* little son into the world."

I was so weak, so tired!

That was all the prayer I prayed for myself, but many, many times I prayed that prayer.

"Give me strength at my son's birth."

The burdened minds of those poor sick children, although old in years as some were. They were all children of Our *father*, sick with the sickness of death and hell.

The old lady:

One afternoon a sweet, old lady was brought to the Old Grist Mill. She was dressed in lovely and becoming clothing. She was eighty-four years old and sent there by her children.

If that sweet, gentle mother had not been murdered on her first day there, I know she would have quickly died of a broken heart.

She was undressed out of her lovely costly clothing, which she never needed again. At supper time which was a little later, she had been put to bed in the same dormitory where Caro, a friend, and I had beds.

While the attendants were out of the room, a large moron, cruel and very strong, attacked this sweet lady kicking her on the spine, sitting on her prostrate body and beating her with her fists. I could not help the dear helpless one because of my unborn son, whose birth was near, but ran to get help. When help came it was too late. She lived probably two hours afterward and died in my arms.

As she lay dying in agony, this lady did not condemn anyone, not even her children, but cried out in sadness:

"Oh, my children, my children, how could you do this to me?"

Then she would call the Lord, saying, "Oh, Lord, *turn your hand, turn your hand.*"

Caro and I went to my bedside and knelt praying for her. Suddenly, the proud lady came and saying nothing to Caro, but yelled harshly at me.

"Get up from there and don't let me ever see you on your knees again, or I'll have you kicked to your feet!"

After she left, off duty for the night, I went back to the dying lady's bed and held my arms around her, trying to comfort her as long as she could hear. The proud one did not interfere. I do not know if the attendants got a doctor for this sweet old lady, whose name I never learned, but if they did it was during the few minutes I was away from her.

After the proud lady ordered me never to kneel and pray in hell, I learned to pray standing or sitting, but still I knelt to pray when she could not see me. Or I would pray lying in my sleepless bed, but my prayers were imperfect then—*my* Lord taught me how to pray afterward.

The morning following the death of the old lady, Caro was sent to what was known as the "Best Cottage," where my kind doctor friend afterward transferred me during the month of August. There our friendship was renewed.

"You can't have friends here. You are out of the world here," the authorities told me many times, and tried in every way to make it so.

It was all monotonous, all ghastly!

Caro and I often talked about my unborn son. She loved him and hoped to see him when he was born. She was sent to the cottage, and never did see him.

Caro was a pretty and sweet young woman of thirty-two, the mother of a little girl of nine years. Under pretenses of having a man come to see about buying their home, her crafty husband brought an unscrupulous doctor to see Caro and thence signed away her freedom, testifying that she was insane.

Caro's daughter was taken by her father to a Roman Catholic school where in the time that followed he poisoned her mind against her young mother who loved her so much. She never succeeded in having her daughter with her ever again.

Caro wrote many of the things of the Lord which I gave her. She believed in James and me, and, although she never met him, did not believe that we were insane. Neither did she condemn us.

She had a dear mother, loving and faithful, often sent her little gifts, and always trying to effect Caro's release from hell. To my knowledge, Caro was never mistreated, and had perfect health. Caro's mother finally succeeded in getting her released the month after I went home. She was there in that place one month before I was. Long, long after that terrible time I met Caro once, but she was all for the world then.

I cannot describe all the "patients" for many came, then some went quickly—I do not know where. There were many buildings, and a number of cottages in this hell, or I should say comprising the outward hell. Inside thousands of unfortunates, for whom there were not nearly enough beds, were packed in close proximity. People came faster than they died, and may lay on the floor or on benches. My bed too, almost all the time I spent in hell, was a mattress on the floor, very close to others.

Then April ninth came, a lovely, bright morning. At 9:30 A.M. a lovely thing was given me to write. Mercy had given me a small piece of light colored paper, when I told her I had something to write. Toilet tissue or wrapping paper was all I ever had to write my songs and poems on while there. The proud lady brought me a pencil and paper many times saying, "Write," but I always answered her, "I have nothing to write." And I had nothing to write for her curiosity.

The stub of a pencil and things of the Lord's blessed gift, I kept in the pocket of my kimono. It was an inside pocket, and the fullness of the garment kept them from sight. Certainly the people who washed my kimono would have seen the pocket, but disobeying one of the rules that no one should wash anything, I took the yellow, ill smelling soap, which I secreted from my bath days, and at night washed my kimono when all were in bed, or in cells. Mercy knew I did this but did not tell. My wet kimono I put underneath my mattress to dry as best it could. I also put my "treasures" there, while in bed, taking them out when I dressed.

We went around the circle that morning, the last time for me at the Receiving Cottage I took the little poem I had written in my hand, rolled into a tiny roll, not knowing why. Then I saw James with other men carrying new beds to a nearby cottage. He saw me at the same time and I started walking toward him. How glad I was to see him, for he looked well and walked briskly about the work.

Immediately two guards, who took us outside, starting running to grab me. But just before they reached me I dropped that tiny roll into the grass. James watching me, saw it fall, but they did not. We were so happy to see each other. He spoke to me and I answered him, which we had been told we never should do. That we never should meet or speak to each other again.

Then the guards seized my arms, and dragged me away. My punishment for doing this was keeping me in, out of the fresh air and sunshine for those fifteen minutes, and it was sixty-eight days before I walked around the circle again, and then from the first, lowest hell. That was the third day after being sent there by the proud lady. After this ninth day of April I could not see James, only at a distance through the barred windows, my penalty for my disobedience in speaking to him.

In those earlier days of April, before the ninth, when we were walked around the circle, I used to lie down in a large trough during the five minutes of resting we were allotted before being taken inside. The trough was wide, low, clean and made of wood. It was dry, and I never knew why it was there although it was a blessing for me. I could lie down in the trough, for which I was grateful, and it was not harder than the mattress and pillow provided all of us there.

I wrote this lovely poem one morning, in early April.

GIFT OF GOD

Were we alone, O love, just you and I, with God

Beneath the soft blue sky, beneath some forest tree,

A bed of leaves you'd make for me, and there our child
    would lie;

Cradled on this heart of mine, cradled in those tender arms

Of thine—God's precious gift to me and thee.

His pure eyes, love, blue as thine, filled with the light of God,

Would upon us shine, *his* life a bond of unity and peace of God

'Tween thee and me—a benediction, holy, sweet,

While we bow low at Jesus' feet.

Today, dear one, in prison drear,

Thou art alone and I am here,

Alone you mourn; alone mourn I, behind these bars,

I view the sky, the blessed babe rests near my heart,

Of thee, my love, my life a part.

His birth is near, the child God promised in *his* Love.

I know you'll share with me the agony

That will *his* promise prove. I know your tender heart

Doth grieve alone in pain and shame,

But, O, beloved, glorified when Jesus comes again.

I know you say with me, today, "Thy *will*, O God, be done."

And when 'tis finished, we shall have the *gift of* God,

His son.   *April 9th, 10 A.M.*

One morning the train brought a large, strong woman to the old "Cow Barn." She was more like a man in looks and her voice, the voice of a man. She had a large, evil face; a mind filled with lewdness; and weighed probably two hundred and fifty pounds. Her family visited her frequently as the days passed by, five usually coming at a time. This was her husband and four grown children, for she was elderly.

This woman would not wear any clothes, and entirely nude she would stand at the barred windows in plain sight of men working below, sweeping walks, or working in the shrubbery.

"I am Jesus Christ," she would yell loudly as she danced around. Then a stream of obscenity and vile curses came out of her mouth.

Not long did she stay large or strong looking. She wasted away and was put into a strait jacket and secured to a bed in a padded cell. I was sent to wash her face and hands, to comb her hair.

Once she spat directly into my face. Inwardly I shrank from contact with such a wicked creature, but was I not adjudged a wicked woman? This woman was old in years and wildly insane. Every opprobrium was heaped upon me by the people who were my keepers. I waited on this woman with the same patience and kindness that I gave to the more lovable ones, for did not our blessed *master* say, "Be kind to the unruly and unholy."?

The innocent unborn babe I carried, but how could I protect him in this place? Beset by danger every day, every hour, both day and night. You will understand, my dear, kind friend, as you write these things for me, my grief for my babe and my husband for both of whom I prayed constantly day and night; for James was as innocent as I of intentional or willful wrong doing.

The large, strong woman wasted away, became very, very ill. Her family were sent for, and remained but a little while. That night she died.

Soon after that, I was wondering how she, who was so strong, so short a time ago, had so quickly passed away.

"What did that woman die of?" I asked the proud one.

"Syphilis," was her answer.

"And you had me care for her, and she spat in my face? You exposed my baby to such a terrible thing!"

"She didn't have it then."

But if she did not have the disease on her arrival, and no visitors except her immediate family, no care from the outside, how could she die of such a disease after only a few weeks in that place? The only explanation that could be given would be that she was inoculated with syphilis in that place. But of course I believed she had it when brought there. And this proud enemy of mine knew the facts of which she could not have been ignorant, for she was in charge of hundreds of unfortunates. I had fed that woman the foods they gave me to feed her. I did not change her bed nor wash her body, but washed her face, her hands, and combed her hair. Surely my child and myself were exposed, but we had God's protection.

When I was too weak and near the time of my son's birth, I could no longer care for the physically or mentally ill. I was then given the work of taking care of the "parlor" as they called the room where visitors met their unfortunate ones. It was a large room and I was very weak and tired. So weary of that terrible place, those seemingly endless days and nights. Yet glad that each day was bringing nearer the birth of my son.

Doctor C.:

She had no right to the title of doctor, for she had violated every decency of her profession. She was a drug addict and there for the cure. Instead of being treated as a patient, she was seemingly given the freedom of the place. Even of the "treatment room," the place where all the medical supplies were kept and patients were taken inside of for certain treatments.

The doctors and attendants comprising the staff of the Receiving Cottage talked with this woman as if she were on the same level as they. Her old, wrinkled face, neck and arms, her legs which she so freely showed, all bore great scars like burns from her own manipulation of the needles she had used to satisfy her craving. She had a filthy mind, one of the vilest I ever met with. No human being could contain a mind more vile. Her vulgarity, her extreme obscenity was searing in my ears.

Why did I hear it? Because there was no escape, only a few feet of distance to walk, then iron bars. Her voice was so strident, so loud, for she was unashamed, even proud that she was so. One morning the proud lady told her of a very serious operation to be performed that morning.

"Oh, I wouldn't want to miss that! I'd rather witness a good operation than to eat a fine breakfast. I love to see the blood run," she exclaimed.

The beastly creature licked her large, loose lips as if in anticipation, as if she were going to drink that blood.

One day I was left alone with this old drug addict doctor. Except for the bedfast ones, all others were outside for a little walk going around the circle. I was not permitted to walk with the others since I had spoken to James, and perhaps could not have gone anyway, for I was very weak. My son's birth was near. This vile creature went into the treatment room and came out with a teaspoonful of colorless liquid.

"Swallow this," she commanded, sitting down beside me.

"I'm not taking any medicine."

"But you are taking this."

Knowing it was useless to protest (I could not struggle with a maniac), I took the medicine into my mouth hoping she would turn around or move away, so that I could relieve myself of it. But no, she sat there never taking her eyes from my face, staring directly into my eyes.

At last I swallowed it, praying to God to protect my unborn son and myself, and knowing that Jesus said, "*If ye drink any deadly thing, it shall not hurt you.*" Mark 16:18. I knew that if I drank any deadly thing boastfully, temptingly, it would kill me; but when I knew that I could not protect myself, I believed my Lord would protect me. Always thinking of my baby, I was anxious, but our God did not let that drug hurt him or me. She sat there, staring at me for at least ten minutes, then left me alone.

Why did she do this? I had no way of knowing.

Why did they let a creature so beastly, so depraved as this, have the freedom of the treatment room and the very drugs endangering lives? I had no one to confide in then, or there, so this incident was not mentioned by me. The last news I ever heard of this vile person was years later, that she was the head of a sanitarium for women in that same state. The leopard cannot change his spots; but this creature seemed to accomplish the impossible, although I am sure the spots were still there in her being, but whitewashed outwardly. Doctor C. was one of the devil's most potent imps in hell.

Here, my friend, I will tell you of the "forced" feeding with which James and I were both threatened while we were in hell. A rubber container with a long tube attachment, containing a thin, horrible looking mixture supposed to be milk and eggs, was used. (Stale eggs, probably, and discarded milk.) Taking that tube, an attendant forced it up one's nostril until blood came out, then the mixture was poured into the throat through the nose.

Years ago I remember hearing someone say, "They made him pay through the nose." In hell the inmates paid in suffering through the nose.

The day the proud one threatened to forcibly feed me, I knew it was no use to resist that or anything else they proposed to do. I had seen ten strong people subdue one weak one by throwing the one assailed to the floor, sitting on her and then when she was trussed up, pouring that horrible mixture down her throat.

Before my son's birth I saw this operation performed on seven women in a padded cell. Taking them one by one, they began with the one on the bed. I had carried dressings for this woman when the nurse had dressed her sore, one day. It was in the fleshy part of her hip, which was not fleshy then; it reached the bone and was pus filled. Horrible to see, with its deep rim of red around it. She had syphilis, I was told, and she died very soon after my child was born.

Then, without rinsing that terrible tube, it was forced up the noses of the six in succession, one after another held by overpowering strength. These six women were in seemingly good health but had refused to eat. The rule for this was: if one refused food three times they were forcibly fed.

I stood near the door and watched this sadistic performance. No one told me to go away, and the door was open. It was on the floor where I worked and slept. One, a young woman of twenty had refused to eat and also refused to work. She would not touch a polisher nor would she even make her own bed. She was well and strong, but she refused even to speak. Not once did the attendants cleanse that tube; not once did they run water over it. From the nostril of that horribly ill patient, that tube forced without washing into nostrils of the six apparently healthy working slaves.

A few days later I saw Edith, the young girl who was fed that day. She was standing and the mucous was running copiously from mouth and nostrils. Poor Edith! I do not know whether she had anyone to care. This was so soon before the birth of my son that I do not know what happened to Edith afterward, during the long weeks I lay helpless in bed.

Did I want that experience? Oh no. I wanted to die after my child was safe, but not a lingering death.

But my dear, I want to go back to that first night in hell, to tell more about that seemingly lovely place offered James and me. We learned then that there we must shed our blood, not naturally but spiritually. We suffered death, as spiritual death in hell.

We paid a full price.

Our blood was shed in hell as we were chosen out of all this world and were willing to suffer shame for *his name's* sake. Had James and I been rich and high in this world, darlings of fortune, we would not have been chosen. Had we been learned in theology, and all the religions of this world had been our delight, had we been making merchandise of God's *words*, had we been making our *father's house* a den of thieves, *he* would not have chosen us.

James and I loved *him* with all our hearts, minds, souls and strength. Him only we desired to serve. In those months of freedom, so long ago, before being sent to hell, we never said to each other, "I love you; I desire you." We desired the *kingdom* of God and *his* righteousness, not knowing what the *kingdom* of God was. Not knowing what the righteousness of God was, no how to find it either.

We did not know the *way* to take, so blindly we went to the slaughter. He chose the weak things of the world, the foolish things and the base things (we were all these things in the minds of our enemies) to bring to this perishing world the *truth* and *life* so long hidden away by the enemies of Jesus Christ, our God, our *Savior*. All the shame that crushed our little son's life must be taken away. We gave our lives for Jesus Christ, and *he* gave *his life* to the world. He has given us the understanding and *power* to manifest that *light* that all may be free from superstitions and lies of false teachers, of those who make merchandise of our *father's house*. Free from those who sell oxen and sheep and doves, which they are selling to this day.

Who has tried to show them the *way* out of the wilderness? They think they know, but they do not realize that they are in bondage of Egypt. They say they are "rich and have need of nothing" knowing not that their nakedness will soon be revealed.

It is written, "*Though your sins be as scarlet, I will make them like snow*." Mark 16:18. James and I know that so well, having gone through the fire to have our blind eyes opened. We were just foolish enough to believe the *scriptures* **literally**, not knowing what they meant until we passed the test of fire, of the Jordan, of the Red Sea, of the wilderness.

This world has not searched the *scriptures* daily in the knowledge that there is something to be found by searching. But they have "*heaped to themselves teachers having itching ears*." 2 Timothy 4:3. Jesus repeatedly spoke in parables in the *words* of the Gospel of this most precious *thing* hidden.

Someone found *it* and paid the price of their lives for *it*, because *it* has a price far greater than this world could pay.

It has been paid for them who know *him* not, but they have the price of what their minds contain of "vain traditions," false teachings and a tissue of lies. They say, "Jesus paid it all and there is nothing to pay." I have heard them say it many times.

It is not true.

The *cross* of Christ is worth more than this world could think. His blood is something they have never touched. There is a way to know.

Those who knew and lived *his life* and taught it, were all murdered long ago, and God chose two humble people who love all humanity enough to suffer for *him*, and for them, to know the things of God hidden for ages and *revealed* at this time. Belief, repentance and obedience to *his living word* is required.

Who knows how it can be accomplished but they who paid the price to know?

As Paul said, "*I have fought a good fight; I have kept the faith, I have finished my course.*" 2 Timothy 4:7.

Although I was "praying without ceasing" I learned afterwards when *he* taught me, that I did not know how to pray at that time. Because I did not understand the *scriptures*, only in part, until I had suffered. The *scripture* says of our *master*, "*Jesus learned to obey through the things he suffered.*" Hebrews 5:8. It must have had to be so with James and me.

Now I know the things that were hidden from me then by that "*veil that is over all the earth*" spoken of by Prophet Isaiah. The prayer as recorded fully and perfectly in Matthew sixth chapter is the prayer of faith. And the prayer recorded in John seventeenth chapter shall be fulfilled, *for God will not fail to answer the prayer of his son.*

Although many centuries have passed since that marvelous prayer was prayed, it is just as true today. It's potency has grown in power and strength, through the *blood* of the *lamb*; through the blood of the millions of murdered holy people. Blood-washed true and faithful martyrs to *his* glorious *name*, Jesus Christ.

You who say you love *him*, search *his words*. Believe the Gospel, repent with all your fearful and faint hearts, obey *him*. Hear to one who can show you *his body, spirit* and *life*, as *revealed* through *his name* and to them by the *words he* spoke—*words* of *spirit* and *life*.

It was about two weeks before my baby's birth, that the attendants let me stay in bed one day, for I was so very weak. Also in bed at the same time was another young woman, a quadroon. She was very nice looking. She was expecting a child to be born soon after my son. Suddenly, when the other "patients" were walking around the circle, food trays were brought to us. Perhaps the reason I was included in this sudden attention was because my skin coloring was now rather blue, for the diet was not sufficient.

When the young woman saw the tray given me, she said she wanted it too, although hers had more food on it than mine. However, her attention was diverted by the arrival of the proud lady, so I ate the food after all. I didn't care, I would have given her all the food, for I didn't ask for it and didn't expect it.

The proud lady treated this young woman as if she were an equal, laughing and conversing about her baby soon to come. Neither paid any attention to me, which was just as well, for I had nothing to laugh about in those days of pain and imprisonment. My laughs when I could laugh, were for suffering, unhappy ones there whom I wanted to encourage.

The authorities had erected what they called a sleeping porch, a new annex to the Receiving Cottage which was to contain about sixty-five beds. This was supposed to help alleviate all the crowded conditions. One bed was placed there for the old drug addict doctor and one for me to occupy.

"I am living in the red light district," the old doctor laughingly said, just as we were going to move into this new sleeping porch.

This was because bars had not been placed on windows and red lights were all around, against, and outside the porch. I wondered if she had not lived in a real red light district at a former time.

This new place was more airy and there were no bed patients there, but I was only there for only about one week, the week before my son's birth.

Our letters must be left unsealed. Those in charge put them in the envelopes, if they did, and mailed them for us. When visitors came there were always attendants near, listening to every word spoken. Besides all that, I was "madly insane," they said, many, many times. Even on the day the regular attendants were gone out, and had previously told me to get a specimen for the doctor, as they always do with an expectant mother. As I tried to do so, a young woman attendant almost struck me in anger when she asked what I was going to do.

"I have to get a specimen for the doctor."

"That's a lie! You're crazy!"

I answered her not a word, but there was no specimen for the doctor that day.

"How far is heaven from hell?"

We must go through hell to get to heaven," I said to James on that April day the year before.

But neither James nor I knew why I spoke those words. Neither James nor I knew anything about heaven, or hell, at that time. To know, we had to experience it for ourselves. We did know that in the eyes of the common law and in the eyes of the people we were transgressors. My dear friend, we know now, for we had the experience, and anyone who will hear, may freely have our knowledge without money.

"It takes all kinds of people to make a world," someone once said.

Truly, hell is a world to itself.

Mothers, how would you, adoring the little life within your body, a tortured body, how would you like to spend the last four and one half months of being with child in such a place? How could you bear to give birth to your son there?

No matter what you think, this woman was not insane; never had been and never would be so.

At last came the second of May. At 10:00 that night the Lord gave me a sign. Arising from the bed I walked into the hall where often dear little Mercy had welcomed me. Marie's chair was vacant, for she was busy elsewhere, so Mercy told me to sit there with her. She was sewing and we talked. At midnight, Marie went to her supper and when she returned to duty Mercy would go to eat.

This night of May second, was the one silent night in the Receiving Cottage. The stillness was unbroken by the terrible sounds of every other night I experienced there. One other silent night came later in the lowest hell. I did not tell Mercy of the imminent birth of my son. We sat in perfect silence until seemingly from far away came music, sweet music of harps, but growing nearer and stronger until it was there all around us.

Marvelous music of heavenly hosts, heralding the birth of my son, James's son, God's *promise*. No one could hear that marvelous music but me, I thought.

"Do you hear the music?" I asked Mercy anyway.

"Yes," she answered. "It is not earthly music."

So there was a witness. Another woman heard that music ages ago, and her son was born in a stable as was mine.

Joyful, worshipful music!

Then it faded away, even as it had come.

There was no radio, no television to bring to that dark and cruel hell the comfort of music at midnight, or any morning, noon or evening. While the music was there I wanted to dance, as did Miriam, so joy filled was my soul; but even with only little Mercy as an audience, I felt my swollen body would look hideous. Afterward, all through those hours of agony, I wished I had danced before the Lord, for *he* would not have thought me hideous.

Immediately after the silence which followed the receding music, a terrible pang pierced me like the thrust of a sword.

Mercy took me, locked me into a padded cell, and called the doctor who officiated on that ward, with the woman doctor.

"It will be a long time," was his decision following his examination. Then he promptly left.

Mercy spoke a few kind words to me, then locked the cell.

From 1:00 in the morning until 7:00 A.M. I prayed to my *heavenly father* for strength to bring forth the son *he* had promised me three years before. Through agony never ceasing until my tortured body, even my hair, was dripping cold, cold water, and nausea retched my stomach seven times.

Long hours, lonely hours in which it seemed even God had forsaken me. It seemed that I must die and my body be my son's tomb. No one came near me until 6:00 A.M., then Mercy came and helped me a little, but the suffering was terrible all through those black hours. There was no water to drink, nor was there any light in that cell but the faint glow of the hall light at a distance through the barred "peep-hole" in the door.

At almost 7:00 A.M., two young nurses hearing my agonized calling on *my* God for help, came running to me. One stayed while the other ran to call the doctor and the proud lady.

Until they came, no one touched me, so my son was born with no human help but by *him* alone.

It was the seventh day of the week, at seven in the morning. He weighed just seven pounds. The hour of his birth, and his weight were told me later by Mercy.

The date I knew; it was the third of May.

Mercy also told me my son was born with a veil over his face, and could not breathe until the veil was severed. He was what they call a dry birth.

"Don't hurt my little son," I said, as the proud lady started to take him away. "He is God's son." No one needed to tell me the child was a son.

As my baby was taken away by the proud lady, a hard chill so severe it shook that hard iron bed as it shook my body, struck me. Then someone gave me hot, strong black coffee to drink, which came up immediately The red-haired doctor then came, and taking both of her strong fists pummeled my abdomen as if it were a punching bag, very roughly and without a word for my suffering.

She left me alone and in came, at once, Miss _____, the New England spinster who had so often tried to humiliate and insult me. She sat on a chair before the narrow bed.

"Miss _____, why is it so dark?" I asked.

I could see only an indistinct blur of her white hair and white uniform.

"It is not dark. It is a bright, sunny day," she answered.

I was blind.

From 1:00 A.M., while I was in labor, until about 1:00 P.M., after the birth I was in darkness. From 7:00 A.M., when my son was born, until almost 1:00 P.M., total darkness.

Something unusual must have happened to my tortured body during labor to leave me hovering between life and death, for not long before my son's birth, everything within me seemed to suddenly give way. I knew later that the blood vessels burst and hemorrhaged in my legs, and my body was left torn and in an irrepairable condition from the excruciating pain of bringing forth my son.

Finally, at 1:00 P.M. the Lord raised me up and it was daytime to me. Miss _____ left her "death watch" over me, as the proud one came in the room with a young nurse.

The proud lady took me by my head, the girl took my feet, then my body, my back, so full of pain, was suspended without support. Down the hall they took me, to a hard bed with the head of the bed only a few inches from the always open doorway (for there was no door to close) of the toilet. This toilet was used by one hundred women, or almost that number, day and night. There was no lid to the bowel, not even a top circle.

The foot of my bed was toward the room by which everyone went to meals, to work, or to walk around the circle. Many swung on the bed as they went by, which was very painful for me because of my injured leg, the left one being in the worst condition. I could not ask them, "Please don't shake or swing on the bed," they would have laughed and shaken it harder. Too many times I had seen the reaction of the insane when oppressed by others. There had been no mercy shown them by those over them, and they would show no mercy to the weaker ones.

How could they know pity? They slept not much, they fought much on the slightest provocation, sometimes without provocation at some imagined wrong or slight. They made the black hours of the night hideous with their shrill yells, until their cries were stifled with pillows and chloroform.

How often the scent of chloroform filled that fetid air!

I was very, very ill, but God delivered me. All the medicine they brought me during my stay in bed, I took into my mouth, then into the towel they let me have under the pillow. No one ever knew.

On the third day after my son's birth the red-haired doctor came into the ward and sat on the opposite bed.

"What are you going to call your baby?" she asked.

"Three years before he was born God promised him to me, telling me to call his name Jesus."

"Oh, that won't do; we can't have that. His name will have to be changed," she said.

"His *name* is written in the *lamb's book of life*, and you can't change it," I said.

She is the same doctor who said, four and one half months before, "I guess she is right about her condition." When I told her she could not change my baby's name she went out, saying nothing more to me.

Mothers, do you know how blessed you are when a little babe is delivered into your arms? Do you know what a miracle has been performed? But how would you like to be locked in a cell among the damned in hell and not be able to see your baby's little feet? Not be able to lift him in your arms? Just to lie helpless on your back for three weeks and have just three weeks to look on his face at intervals of four hours for twenty minutes each?

So to James and me was born a son in the place the nurses and attendants always spoke of as the Old Cow Barn.

The proud one always brought my son to me to nurse by day, whether to see my face stained by tears which flowed day and night, or to see and taunt me for the joy in my eyes when my darling was laid in my arms. Knowing that soon my son would be taken from me as she threatened to put me on one of the back wards where, she said, "No one ever knows what goes on there."

"If you don't quit going around with that martyr look, I'll put you on a back ward and adopt your child out," were the words she said to me many times.

She would have taken my baby from me if she could have done so.

Of my son I had said at his birth, "Do not hurt my little son, for he is God's son," and still say. For God promised him, *he* gave him, and without God he would have had no being. How sweet he was! His little lips touched my breast as if caressing me. His tiny hands lay on my breast. My son! For whom I prayed. God's son, the son of promise.

Miss ____, the elderly New England nurse, a spinster, in her righteousness taunted me frequently with what she called my "shame" before my baby was born.

"I am not ashamed." I always told her. "For God gave James to be my husband."

"If you knew a young girl who was expecting a child before marriage, would you despise her?" she once asked me.

"No, I would be very sorry for her," I answered.

I told her that James and I had been joined together for the fulfillment of God's *will*. No one could shake my belief. No one but God could change me one iota. I had promised to drink the *cup* for *him*; I had promised to serve *him*, had forsaken all that I had for *him*. What I had given up was dearer to me than my heart's blood.

Not for any man did I do this thing, but to obey *him* which gave me *commandment*.

Being a natural woman without understanding of the *scriptures*, before my son's birth, believing him to be spoken of in the *scriptures*, all of which I took literally, I expected him to be "caught up to God and to *his* throne" when he should be three days old. But when this was not done, I did not blame God for what I found was just my ignorance of understanding *his words*. I had believed that our son's father, James and myself would be naturally killed there. But found it was a far worse death and agony, long drawn out, which when accomplished set us free from all the misunderstandings, false hopes, all the errors of ages since the true *church* was martyred by the evil powers. It has been *revealed* and the world must be told the "glad tidings."

"If we had gotten you a little sooner, you would not have had this baby." The proud lady said to me.

But God knew James and I had to go through the way that made us a natural mother and father, so we could know "that which is spiritual is not first, but afterward that which is spiritual." There had to be a natural son born to us before our blind eyes could be opened to know the spiritual and *eternal son* of God. All the things told me years before our child was conceived, I understood to be told of my baby. I could not know that which must be brought forth at this time is, was and forever shall be, *the word of* God, *his only begotten son.* **The words** *spoken* by Jesus.

Mary A.:

A few days after the birth of my son, Mary A. was brought in one day on the afternoon train. She was not locked in a cell, as was the custom or rule of the place, as I had been.

She was permitted to eat in the room we had our meals, and to sleep in the dormitory where one hundred and perhaps twenty had beds. About sixteen of these were bed patients or too insane to be allowed outside a padded cell. After supper that evening, Mary passed my bed as did all the others who walked, to go to the small toilet room used by the unfortunates day and night.

She stopped by my bed, and leaned over me and my son, then just a few days old. My head was on the pillow just inches from the doorway which had no door.

"How sweet he is! I have five little ones," she exclaimed.

After a few more words she went back to her bed farther down the aisle, about ten beds from mine.

The next morning when I was again nursing my son, Mary again rose from her bed and tore the strong top off the table which was placed at her bedside. She began to deal blows at the beds and their occupants, beating one strong young woman into unconsciousness and wounding a number of others. Helplessly I lay with my tiny baby and prayed for help. I stretched my weak, wasted arms across his little body, but knew that only God could save him from destruction.

Someone who awakened out of the paralysis of fear, and the terrified calls of the people in the room, brought the nurses running to subdue Mary. Two men then came with a stretcher and carried the unconscious girl out. Long before my release, Mary A. was operated and sent home to her family. Sent home as cured, but never to be an expectant mother again.

When my little son was one week old, Maud was brought to the door by two young nurses who led her by a leather strap. Maud, who bit and fought the nurses, so they said, was let free of the strap and turned loose at the foot of my bed. My precious one was in my arms nursing, and we were both helpless, baby no more than I. But Maud, being left at the foot of the bed that day, looked at the lovely baby and spoke to me.

"Where did you get the little baby?"

"God gave him to me," I said.

Then coming to the side of the bed, dear Maud went on. "Who is he?"

"He is the baby Jesus, your little Savior," I answered; and believed it.

Then dear Maud placed her wasted hands on my baby's head, tears streamed down her colorless, sad face, as she sang in a sweet voice, the beautiful song, "Jesus, Savior, pilot me." She sang it all, and smiling happily she asked God to bless him, and walked away.

Pretty soon the two young women who brought her and disappeared into another room, took the strap and led Maud away. She never needed that strap again; she never needed restraint, for the next morning, word was brought to the Receiving Cottage, and gladly I heard the news being told by the nurses to each other.

"What do you think? Maud is in her right mind! Maud is well!

Glorious news!

That night, my angel nurse mentioned it to me, and I told her what Maud had done the evening before. How happy we were for her.

I had seen the nurses leading Maud by that locked strap, and one day throw her savagely against the wall. The distance they threw her was at least eight feet. I saw this from my bed, for it was in the same dormitory. Maud had one ear almost torn off by the impact and the blood flowed profusely to the floor. They jerked the strap, removing her from the room. The two women were both nurses who did this. Nurses should be angels of mercy; Maud did nothing, only she was not walking fast enough to please them.

The God of *mercy* heard Maud's prayer that day, for Jesus to pilot her. He answered. He performed a miracle. Yes, *he* does many miracles, even in prison and in hell.

When five weeks later I was taken to the same place where Maud had been taken, Maud was rejoicing, Maud was packing her clothes, nice, fine clothes that she had worn long before but not in that place. She was a new creature, with rosy, firm flesh on those gaunt bones, heavy, long, thick curly hair on that once bald head, eyes bright and beautiful, eyes that had five weeks ago been full of pain and despair. Just five weeks from the day she had stood by my bed, her hands on my baby's head, standing with that heavy, locked strap around her waist, those faded rags on her emaciated form, singing, "Jesus, Savior, pilot me." He had indeed taken Maud into the *harbor* of *life*. How happy I was that she was going home.

Covered by pretty clothes were the scars those terrible scars of Maud's body; blotted out of her mind by joys were those dark scars of her mind, replaced by gratitude at being able to go home.

Dear Maud, knew me and put her loving arms around me. Maud, who loved babies could never hold one of her own to her breast and know that from her breast flowed life giving sustenance for her child. She could teach little children and she could help many others. She might have a kind, loving husband. I can only hope and pray that everything she deserves would come to her, for she had suffered so cruelly. I never heard anything more of Maud; nothing of her life which I hoped and prayed was blessed and full of happiness. I know that I loved her and that she loved my God, Jesus Christ, in the best way she knew.

Mrs. M.:

She was a young woman, large and very quiet, sluggish in her movements as if she were crushed by some weight of sorrow too heavy to bear. She used to come and kneel at my knees as if I were her mother, and ask me to pray for her.

"Please pray for me," she would say, putting her hands on my knees, and looking into my eyes. "I want to go home to my family."

I put my hands on her head, poor child! And in pity prayed to our *merciful father*, so that she could hear. One day while I was helpless in bed after my son's birth, I was told that she had attacked one of the women attendants, and had been "restrained" as they call it. I never saw her again. Who knows under what provocation she had attacked the woman, if she did so?

Those six weeks in which I lay helpless in bed, many terrible things went on day after day, but there was nothing I could do to prevent evil or save others from punishment. No, no more than I could help myself. Could I forget through all these years? Could I ever forget the screams of those lost, barren slaves who cried with hands lifted high, "Blood! Blood!" when they saw the red-haired doctor in her blood red car? They had been smothered with pillows and chloroformed, put into hot packs, tortured by kicks, beatings, cruel words and scorn, hated and starved by their own womankind. And they could say to me, "When you go home, you will forget us!"

Never! No, never!

Here I must tell you more of an angel in hell. I call her name Mercy, but that is not her name. That is what she was to me. She and her friend were on night duty and both were kind.

Marie, the friend, was large and blonde. She had no children. Mercy was small with blue eyes and dark hair. Mercy was under average in height and weight, but she was worth her weight in gold. Dear and dainty, precious Mercy. I never heard her speak crossly to anyone, but her job depended on the proud one. I heard that proud lady reprimand her one night.

"If you don't quit favoring that woman (that woman was her name for me) I'll take you off the job and send her to a back ward."

Her threat, made so many times, to send me to a back ward, she fulfilled one day.

Mercy's husband and Marie's husband worked as attendants on the ward to which my husband was taken. They liked James, and neither those two men or their wives believed James or me insane. I did not meet the husbands, but the two young nurses told me of them.

Mercy was the mother of a little son who lived with his grandmother while she worked. I did not see her little boy, for children were never brought there, only children of the imprisoned ones who came with other relatives. After I was released I never saw Mercy again and I was told that she died of pneumonia. A great loss to the sad unfortunates. And she was too young.

Mercy heard that *heavenly* music at midnight on that May night that my son was born. Mercy believed the *name* of our *heavenly father* (Jesus Christ) as it had been *revealed* to me.

Mercy told me one night, as my son lay in my arms nursing on his four hour schedule:

"I always see a halo around your head and around your baby's head whenever he is in your arms."

This was astonishing news to me, but Mercy had seen the halos from the first until the last night my baby was in my arms, for those three short weeks. Sometimes she let me hold him a little longer than the allotted twenty minutes.

The proud one brought my son to me by day and each time she brought him, from the top of his head to the end of his clothing, he was soaking wet, just as if dipped in water.

He was kept in the treatment room, where patients were taken for hypodermics or anything needed—that is, patients who were able to walk there. The diseased were in the same small room where my baby lay, where he spent the days and nights of his stay in hell. He was as if dipped into water because when he cried I know his little cries were hushed by a pillow over his face as the others in that place were smothered to stop their cries.

Never had I wept so much. It seemed the depths of my very being were flooded with tears day and night. To hide them when any of the attendants came near my bed, I pulled the horrid smelling sheet over my face, turning my head aside from them. At night time no one could see those tears I wept, as if I could never weep again.

"See that he nurses and don't let him go to sleep," the proud lady always said when she brought my son to me.

He nursed so daintily, not hungrily as babies do, although his schedule was at four hour intervals. His little lips scarcely seemed to touch my breast; they were like rose petals.

"Why do you cause my innocent little baby to suffer?" I asked the proud one, as his little wet head lay on my arm.

"Oh, he'll have to suffer," she said, and her evil prophecy was being fulfilled.

After he grew into young boyhood, he suffered because of the precious name Jesus by which he was called. Just one, a Jew, a young insurance agent who came to collect; when I handed him my son's book said, "That name will be a great blessing to him and to you."

I was so sorry at the next collection time when another man came and I, asking for this young man, (we had seen him but that one time) received the answer that, "He was fixing a flat tire by the roadside when a hit and run driver left him dead by the car on which he was working." How sad! The agent told me he had taken out insurance in that company a few months before to the amount of fifty thousand dollars. That his wife had abandoned her little ones and himself for another man and having no one else, he then took out the policy for his children and so left them well provided for. But a father is worth more than money and they were fatherless and worse than motherless.

The proud one continued to make threats regarding my son. Now, I must let my tiny son go from me for his own sake, not ever expecting to hold him in my arms again. He suffered much in hell, and I, his mother who adored him, would have spared him even one moment of suffering.

When he was two weeks old, the red-haired woman doctor came in, seating herself on that bed opposite the one on which I lay those first three weeks after his birth.

"Will you allow me to send my baby away from here with my friends?" I asked her during her visit with me.

She looked astonished. I had never told her or anyone how the proud lady persecuted my little one and me.

Holding my breath in fear that she would answer "no," I waited. At last, at long last it seemed to me, she gave her reply.

"Yes, you may send him home with your friends."

I thanked her.

The proud lady came to speak to the doctor, who informed her that I was to write my friends to come for the baby. Immediately the proud one brought paper and pencil to me and I wrote, asking them to please come for my little son on the following Sunday.

So, on Sunday morning, May 25th, the day my son was three weeks and one day old, my two kind friends came to take him away from the Old Cow Barn. The nurses lifted me into a low rocking chair, dragged the chair and me into the same room where I had made my baby's clothes.

Then they let my woman friend come into the room with me. They brought a clean, large, wash basin, the soap I had ordered from my friend, some of the soft cloths I had made for him, and a complete outfit of his little clothes, besides several of his blankets to wrap him in.

The proud lady then brought my son to me, and she placed him in my arms.

"You may bathe and dress him," she said.

What a privilege!

Just once I thought, just once as they planned, to see my son's perfect body, to see his little feet, to hold and care for him, just once. What joy, what bitter sorrow!

The proud one went out locking the door, but my friend was left with me to help, for I had not sat up since the birth and was so weak.

How wonderful to at last really see my son! To hold his little feet; to kiss his sweet body all over; to kiss his pretty, curly, bright gold hair! He was very solemn. He did not know what to think. My tears flowed down my cheeks onto his little, lovely head, body and feet. They helped me bathe him. He was as clear and pure as a pearl, without blemish.

How would any mother feel, to be locked in a room, and have her baby brought to her for the first time to wash and dress?

Such joy to hold him, to see him!

But oh, what sorrow to believe it was for the last time, for I had been told many times there, "You will never get out of here."

Can you imagine the anguish I knew?

After my baby was bathed, I then nursed him until the attendants came.

"Hurry up!" they said.

In the few moments we had left, I asked my friend about the new nursing bottle and nipple she had brought along. She had failed to sterilize them! I knew that the nipples made at that time were coated with a poisonous film, which had almost caused the death of a baby girl.

"Oh this nipple should have been boiled and cleaned. The bottle should have been boiled, too," I told her.

All that I could do was ask her to give me clean, cold water, (which was all we had) from the wash room. I took the water and washed as hard as my weak hands could, then putting the nipple into my mouth, I chewed it over and over, continuing to wash it. I could see that sweet little body, tiny hands and feet, which I had kissed repeatedly and bathed with tears of love and sorrow, suffering from poison!

"As soon as the train stops, get boiling hot water and wash this nipple and bottle before you let my son have it," I instructed my friend.

"I will," she promised.

So, many kisses I gave my lovely darling, and then he was gone. But it was many long weeks of torment before I heard that my baby was well. Oh, the anguish of hell.

Oh, the punishment too heavy to bear, but Jesus Christ was even in hell.

I tried to compose my face and keep back my tears as the nurses dragged me in the chair back to my bed, helped me into it, then left.

I crawled weakly into that malodorous little room, and knelt on my knees, praying and weeping, and resolved that I would never eat another bite of food, so that I should soon die. I wanted to very much.

"Oh, God," I cried. "Surely my punishment is more than I can bear!"

He did not answer me.

"My God, my God, why hast thou forsaken me? I gave up all I had to obey you. Everything I held dear, dearer even than my heart's blood. You gave me my husband, You gave me your *son*, my son, now they are both taken away. Oh let me die, let me die!"

The people were all out, except the bed patients, and no nurse was in sight, so I was all alone. I had not seen James, even at a distance since the 9th of April. There was no help, no hope, only my God who seemed to have forsaken me.

At last, shaking and spent, I dragged myself along the floor back to my hard, cold bed.

Meal time came. I did not eat, and could not have touched that tasteless food if I had been hungry.

Again, at evening they brought the same. I did not touch it.

In the morning food was brought again. But still I did not eat.

No one said anything to me, but presently the proud lady came to the side of my bed with a cup in her hand.

"You know that if you do not eat, we will forcibly feed you," she said.

Yes, I knew how she had helped to feed seven women shortly before my son's birth. I had watched her so proudly holding the container while her satellites forced that slimy tube into nostrils and down throats, without once rinsing it in cold water. I wanted to die, but not that way. That was worse than death.

I said nothing. It was all I could do to restrain my sobs.

"Drink this!" she commanded sharply, and held the cup to my mouth.

I drank. It was buttermilk, the first I had seen there.

I thought of her kindness for bringing it to me, and wondered, did she pity me after all, after all her cruelty?

Two requests I made there, one for my baby that he should be sent home, the other that his father should be permitted to see him. One request for James and myself, that I might be allowed to see my baby's father for a few moments.

These requests I made of the superintendent when he made his first call after my son's birth.

"No," he answered. "James cannot see the child. Neither can you see the baby's father. You can never see each other again."

Another day he came to my bedside to question me.

"Is this child the son of the man who was brought here with you?"

"He is not any man's son," I said. "He is the *son* of God."

God had promised me a son, had named him, had given him even in hell. I knew that James was the father of that little human body; but he was not the father of that *spirit* which gave him; and without the *spirit* my son could not have been.

Truly, as I believed, I answered the superintendent. But the superintendent could not understand my words. Could I blame him for thinking me crazy, to give him the answer he received from me? But he knew that I was not crazy, or insane.

After I had answered him thus, "He is the *son* of God," he turned away angrily and walked from the room.

But, without the knowledge of the superintendant, when the baby was eight days old, Mercy's husband and Marie's husband had taken James to the Receiving Cottage to see and name our son. James took our baby up into his arms, kissed his little head and blessed him.

"What are you going to name your son?" the attendants asked.

"He is already named. His name is Jesus Christ."

Nothing more was said, and James was returned to his ward by these two men who befriended him.

Two weeks later, on the day our son was taken away from hell, these same two attendants again performed a kindness. They took James to the entrance door of the Receiving Cottage, meeting our woman friend and her husband, who had the baby. Then they allowed James to carry our son in his arms to the waiting cart and horses. There he bid our friends "goodbye," and kissed our son for what he also believed to be the last time.

I was told later of these acts of compassion by Mercy and Marie, and it helped to somewhat lighten my burden of sorrow for James.

Later that day when my little son was taken away, I was moved to a bed on the other side of the toilet, with just one bed between me and that odorous place. There I spent the remaining three weeks of my stay at the Receiving Cottage.

All my life I had been sensitive to odors and always will be as long as I live. They nauseate me; but I did not speak of it there. I learned by seeing the effect produced by others, that in that place "silence is golden." Showing disgust at their filthy ways was written on my face. The inmates were almost all insane. Did they think themselves sane? Had they lost the faculty of thinking? Some had, while I knew that I was sane and my mind was clear, clean and alive forever.

In the evening, after my baby was gone, the proud lady came with a young nurse, bringing condiments and astringents, I suppose to dry up the abundant flow of milk. My breasts were filled with milk, almost to bursting and very painful. But the sweet baby lips would never again be held to my breast, and he looked into my eyes, grateful for what I so gladly gave him to sustain his sweet body. He was so lovely.

"Don't give this woman any milk to drink after this," the proud one ordered the nurse.

Then she roughly handled my swollen breasts.

"This woman will never have milk in these breasts again," she continued speaking.

She meant to have me sterilized, as they called it; but no knife was laid upon my flesh nor James's, although he heard them plotting to do so, when they thought him asleep. But this woman came out openly and threatened me often. She hated me with an intense hatred without a cause.

"When your little girl comes...," the proud one often said, before May 3rd, when speaking of my expected baby. But I always replied, "God did not promise me a daughter; He promised me a son. I am going to have a son."

Then after my release, a friend who had come to see James had a conversation with this proud lady.

"We believed that when the baby was born it would be a girl, and one of their delusions would be shattered. But he was one of the finest boys you ever saw," she told our friend.

One day when this proud lady and the same young nurse bandaged my left leg, as they did for six weeks after my son was born, this certain day she began to speak cruelly of my innocent child, too far away now for her to hurt, too young to feel her hate, and to revile his father, calling him vile names. If it had all been against me as was so often the case, I would not have answered a word. I never had responded to her most insulting abuse of me. But my innocent baby, my husband God had given me, to listen to that abuse against them, worse than ever before, I was aroused to speak to her Psalm 72:9.

"They that dwell in wilderness shall bow before him, and his enemies shall lick the dust of his feet."

And Isaiah 49:23.

"They shall bow down to thee with their faces toward the earth and lick up the dust of thy feet, and thou shalt know that I am the Lord, for they shall not be ashamed that wait for me."

"You shall bow down," I told her, "and lick the dust of their feet."

This made her so angry that she took the top sheet and drawing it tightly about my throat, one hand on each side, she drew the sheet so I could not speak.

I was glad, for I thought, "Now she will kill me and I shall be free."

But my Lord spoke in *his* dear *voice*.

"Clap your hands!"

I raised my arms and clapped my hands while tears of joy at the hope of deliverance were flowing down my face. But instead of finishing her murderous act, as I clapped my hands, she loosed the sheet. Then as *he* opened my mouth, and praises to my God poured from my bruised throat and filled the air.

The proud lady could not bear it. Saying not a word, she turned and left the room; the young nurse, with tear filled eyes, following her. So hastily did she leave, that her long, sharp, surgical scissors were forgotten in my bed. I believed that would cause her serious trouble if the higher authorities knew she had left her scissors in the bed of a woman they and she called insane.

But I did what *my master* had taught me, "returned good for evil."

When one of the attendants came near my bed I spoke to her.

"Please ask Miss _____ to come to me," I said.

She came.

"Miss _____ you left your scissors in my bed. They are under my hip."

She reached into the bed and taking them, walked away. But she was no kinder to me than before.

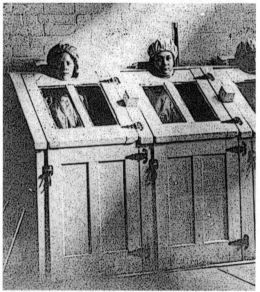

Water therapy was supposed to be beneficial to the patients, but was often used as a torture, by cruel, sadistic attendants and nurses.

Part III
FIRST LOWEST HELL

HELL, THE PLACE OF LOST SOULS OR LOST MINDS

All over the world there are institutions for the insane which contain people who have lost their minds, both of all natural knowledge of man and of spiritual knowledge of God, and have reverted mentally to become as ignorant, raging, wild beasts of prey.

There are countless thousands of these poor people, who have gone back to the state of beasthood, locked up in cells in the pits of hell. Along with these there are more countless thousands, who have been pitifully turned into spiritual beasts by the old religious world's teachings that the *scriptures* must be understood naturally by the spirit of man or the devil (which is all it possesses) instead of spiritually, by the *spirit* of God.

Matt. 8:36-37 *For what shall it profit a man, if he shall gain the whole world, and lose his own soul?*

Or what shall a man give in exchange for his soul?

Job 27:8 *For what is the hope of the hypocrite, though he hath gained, when God taketh away his soul?*

First Lowest Hell

The day I was sent from the Receiving Cottage to the first lowest hell, I was not able to walk, but was told to go, so I went. The bandage had been taken from my leg three days before, but it was not well and I, having gone through the *valley of the shadow* six weeks before the bandage was removed, was so very weak and sad. I had not heard one word of my little son since my friends had taken him away, after his three weeks in hell.

It was on a Monday morning, June 15th, that two trustees came to my bedside.

"We're taking you to an other place," they said.

No other explanation was given. They had my few belongings in a clothes bag of heavy white canvas. I knew that I was unable to walk, having been in bed for six weeks, but the women took my arms, one on the left, the other on the right, and they rushed me through a tunnel of which I had not known existed before.

It did not occur to me until long afterward why they took me through a tunnel. Then I concluded that someone had come to see me that morning, and they hurriedly took me away, perhaps telling them that I was "too disturbed to be seen," as I had known of them doing to others. The proud lady did not make an appearance, but her threat to, "Put you in one of the back wards," was fulfilled.

This place is what I called, "The lowest hell number one." On that first day in the first lowest hell, (where I saw Maud packing to go home) I found it worse than the Old Cow Barn where my son was born. I had thought the horrors of that first place could not be equalled anywhere, but found this was far, far worse. More than double.

On my entrance I was given a supposed bath in a slimy tin tub. These tubs, which were used on all the back wards, were long, narrow, and about eight inches deep. They were removable, always carried out, but seemingly not washed out after use. There was never more than two to four inches of water, and the dark, yellow, fish-oil soap.

After my bath, I was seated on a bench before a bed almost hidden in the end of a corridor. I watched the attendants remove a young woman from that bed, and without changing the sheets or slip, put me into it. What a mockery they made of cleanliness!

My heart, which was pounding so hard all the way over, was chilled at the prospect of lying in that bed. The poor girl who had just left it was covered with syphilitic sores, from her head to her feet. Red angry looking sores. She was nude. You might know that I did not like to get into such a bed, but there was no escape.

The large, young woman was in her twenties:

Her pale, red hair was very scanty, or thin, and cut very short. Perhaps because her festering sores. She was an expectant mother, perhaps eight months along, and she cried sadly day and night.

"Why did I cross the bay? Why did I go to the city?"

She continually repeated these words. Where was the answer?

In a few days, I was at last trusted enough to take this young woman to the Receiving Cottage for treatments. The attendants put a strong, leather strap, locked around her waist. This was long enough for one to lead her just like a dog on a leash. She could easily have escaped from me as I was so weak and undernourished.

The walk, from this hell I was in, was not far from the Receiving Cottage, but there was a bridge half way, a bridge high enough to kill her if she had decided to jump from it. Every time we came to the center of the bridge she stopped still. I always kept silent, praying and tightening my hands, imperceptibly to her, on that leash. I had read that mental cases must think they are having their own way, so I stood patiently while she stopped there.

"Oh, why did I go across the bay that night? Why did I go to the city?" she would say over and over in anguish.

Then she was willing to go on without a word. This was repeated day by day, with always that sad moaning.

Who was she? And had someone beguiled her to go to her destruction by pretending to love her? One could only surmise that she was a nice girl, out for a night of pleasure, given drink, deceived, seduced in the city by an evil creature, who then left her diseased with syphilis and the mother, to be, of a child.

Too many young girls have gone that way. How many are hidden in hell to hide their shame? As soon as this young woman's child was born, she would be operated, so that she could never bear another. This girl was of the more privileged class, but now abandoned to a fate worse than death. Her name was never mentioned. The outcome is unknown to me. I was assigned the task of taking her for treatments, and pitifully, kindly, I did so.

On my arrival at this first lowest hell, I was kept in bed for a few days. Toward morning on that first night, I awoke to find what I thought at first sight was a child of perhaps twelve years. But looking at her in the half light of early morning, coming through those heavily barred windows, I saw she was a young woman. She had short, black, curly hair, lovely brown eyes, dark complexion, and a perfect little form which was completely nude. I was startled, but not too much to question her.

"Why don't you go and get into your bed, honey?"

"I have no bed," she answered.

This I found was true, when I visited the Water Section the next morning. She and others were tied with sheets on top of narrow benches. Nude, and with nothing under them, nothing over them. The feces were running onto the floor from the beautiful, little, brown skinned girl, (she was a Caucasian), sound asleep now on that hard bench, as were the others. Afterward I was told that she had a little boy who burned to death, and sorrow and shock caused her to lose her mind.

About one week after my entrance into this lowest hell, I saw James from the window, and watched him as he worked. How happy I was to see that he was well!

For awhile, after getting out of bed, I was still too ill to push polishers, so was charged with feeding the unfortunates tied in the Water Section. What a place to eat foods! I washed these womens' faces, hands, and helped herd them out to walk around the circle. This was their only liberty, for at all other times they were tied or in strait jackets, according to their state. Other patients, who were bed fast, I cared for by feeding them from trays, and washing their hands and faces.

At this place all heads were washed in a little tepid water with fish oil soap, and what hair they had was all combed with the same comb, as in the Receiving Cottage. Nearly all heads of the women were shorn, but they did not cut my hair which was long, curly and abundant.

The doctor in charge of this first lowest hell was a good, kind man doctor, G.W. He treated me kindly and was my friend, as was the matron on this ward. She was a calm, sympathetic woman who never spoke a harsh word to anyone that I heard. But matron Ann and my kind, dear doctor friend did not know what was done of the cruelty and lies to the poor helpless ones in that place.

The first time I had strength to walk around the circle, I saw James in the distance with other men carrying beds. As I watched, I saw him look at me and then drop a small roll of paper in the brush. I started to go to get it, but two women hastily seized me. matron Ann came and asked what I wanted.

"My husband dropped a letter over there in the brush. I want to find it."

"I'll help you find it," she kindly said, and went with me. I saw it first and picked it up.

"Give it to me," she commanded before I could read it. She read the paper and then handed it back.

"You may have it."

He had just written *scriptures*, nothing else.

Here it was floor polishing, making beds, dusting, caring for the sick and patients brought back from the operating room. It was a hideous place. Death came to many, and horrible and most cruel punishment to many, which I suffered in sympathy.

On July 13th, at 1:00 A.M., I, not having slept, was told by my Lord to go to the window. All was quiet at last.

The terrible noise was stopped. I arose from my mattress on the floor, which was my bed since I recovered my strength, and went to the window as commanded.

There high in the sky was a large, large bell in the act of ringing!

The bell had a rent down its side. I had seen pictures of that "Liberty Bell" many times, but I was seeing it now with my eyes wide open. It was so vivid I thought it was really there, high above the third floor where I was, on this bright, moonlit night.

As soon as it was daylight I went to the window and looked again, but the bell was not there. It had been a sign from God. But as I looked this time, there was a vision of a man and woman on a raised dias. A babe was on the woman's breast; then the baby changed to a pure white lily with a golden heart.

When I saw this, in my ignorance of understanding God's *message*, I thought my son was dead. More grief to bear in hell! For seven long weeks passed after my son was taken away before I heard from my friends about him.

"He is well and he is so good," they then said.

I had not known whether he had lived or died.

A former French Madame:

She was extremely vile in her speech and actions, addicted to vile cursing, and card playing. Yes, they could play cards or gamble, they could curse and speak all kinds of filthy words; but no one could have a Bible nor pray where they could be seen in hell. This one, like the old drug addict doctor, had the freedom of the place, going into the grounds early in the morning. I saw her many mornings from the barred windows of my prison. She seemed to come and go as she chose and no one ever reproved her, to my knowledge. She was very loud and exceptionally lewd. She could have told of all those evil practices if she wished, but she was one of the devils in hell.

The aristocratic French woman:

There was another old French woman in the lowest hell, but she was an aristocrat. The attendants said that she was a millionairess, and that her husband had brought her there years before to die, for he wished her dead.

"How come you to be alive yet? I put you here to die," he exclaimed when he came to inquire about her after several years.

The attendants brought out the old woman into the visiting room as visible proof that she was alive. But, regardless of the husband's desire, she was too profitable to the institution, for a great sum of money was paid for her room, board and care.

The first time I saw the aristocratic French woman, we were sent down from our third floor ward in the "chute," an augur-shaped slide that was used instead of the stairway when going downstairs. She was very large and heavy, nearly eighty years old and weak. Neither she nor I knew how to go down the chute, but she landed in a heap We were ordered to stand on a little platform at the top in small groups, then suddenly, without warning, we were dropped into the chute to whirl dizzily down the slide to the bottom.

At the bottom, a large young moron roughly pulled this old woman around the circle. Then we went inside the door on our return, the same moron took this weak old woman by her soft white hair, and cursing her, dragged her forcibly upstairs by her hair.

That was a sample of the old lady's care.

After that first day I saw this old lady I made myself her helper, and gently led her, talked to her kindly, even if she could not understand. For she spoke only French, of which language I knew nothing. She did understand my actions, however.

Her food? I fed her the same coarse, horrible food served on the table, cold as always. I fed her because her poor old hands were tied so she could not do anything for herself. I peeled the black from her small portion of potatoes. I fed her from the tin plate with the tin spoon. The place where I had to feed her was the Water Section, where the drinking faucets and open toilets were continually being used.

This woman and others were tied to hard, bare benches at night, and all day, and only released when taken around the circle to walk. Is it any wonder they were weak? Starved, beaten, kicked, dragged by the hair—oh, the cruelty of hell! There was a cover under some of their bodies on the floor, at night, put there to protect the floor and benches from emanations; but never any covers over them. Day and night I went into that place and saw them there.

I met Ila again on this ward in this first lowest hell.

"This is hell!" were the words she greeted me with.

No one was more cruelly treated in hell than was Ila, to my knowledge; but it may have been because she, being supposedly in her right mind, continuously exasperated the attendants. Every time one came near her, she would clasp them around the legs and hold fast.

"Oh, I want to go home! I want to go home!" she would cry as they beat her off.

"My family is at the beach and I am here in this hot place suffering with intolerable heat! My family has all nice clothing and foods and here I'm dressed in these old faded rags and I'm starving," she would wail other times.

There was no pity shown her. I begged her to be calm, to obey the rules. She never wanted God or a Bible, as I; she never said, "I miss my loved ones, I'm lonely for them." No, this high born lady was the most selfish person I ever saw or knew. There was no reason why she should disobey them if she wished to go home. Every day I was so distressed to witness her punishment.

"Ila," I would say, "do what they tell you, and very soon they will let you go home."

And they would have, if the Lord had so willed it. She poured all her complaints into my ears, but she would not hear a word I spoke to her. I thanked God that no word of unkindness was spoken to her by me.

Ila used to swing on gentle matron Ann's clothes, holding fast, or around her waist also crying to her.

"I want to go home!"

But the matron never spoke an angry word to Ila or anyone, no matter how trying they were. Ann would gently disengage her hands and speak softly to her.

"Ila, I wish I could help you go home."

One afternoon matron Ann was down in the yard directing men who were bringing beds, which were badly needed. I was one of the many who slept on a mattress on the floor. High above the yard Ila and I were watching the work from the window through the bars. Suddenly Ila, her face distorted with hate, made the motion of drawing a gun.

"If I only had a gun I would kill her," she said.

My heart, for the first time was turned away from Ila for her murderous desire.

"Oh, she is not to blame," I said. She is good to everyone."

"I hate her! I hate her! Ila cried.

It was useless for me to say anymore. Later that afternoon, that hot afternoon, when the attendants came and found Ila was nude, they threw her on her bed. Then taking off their sharp heeled shoes, they both beat her furiously on her head, her face, her body and limbs, bare to the fury of their onslaught. Ila writhed and screamed in pain until, unable to control, she flooded her bed with urine. This made her attackers even angrier still.

"We'll fix you," they cried.

They carried out their threat that hot night. I wondered what excuse was made to the relatives and what was said by the coroner when he saw that body? I never heard anything about it, but the next morning the attendant was asked by one of the patients.

"Where is Ila?"

"Ila has gone home," she answered.

Poor, wasted life!

Night after night and day after day, poor Ila had been tortured in hot packs in a small, locked room, where no one could give her ice water or any water to drink, or for her burning head. No one who cared could help her. This was done to her until the last day which was one of those hot days in July which reached 104 degrees.

My bed was, as usual, on the floor beside others and very near the door, so that anyone entering that door passed within two feet of me. Also, as usual, I was not sleeping. It was one of the two nights of quiet in hell, the other was the night my son was being born.

"Water! Water!" I heard Ila cry. "I want a drink of water." The nurse attendant paid no heed to her cries.

I prayed, over and over as once I had prayed long ago for myself, "God have mercy on my soul!" But this night I prayed for Ila, over and over again.

"Oh, God have mercy on her soul!"

Her cries grew more pleading.

"Give me water, I'm dying, I'm dying!" growing ever fainter.

Still no help.

I could not help; I had no keys. Mercifully I fell asleep and it was early. Never had I slept there at all before early hours of the morning. All at once I awoke, just one sound I heard, the sound of low sobbing. It was 10:00 P.M.

"Ila is dead," I said to myself

Why was the nurse sobbing? She had not answered those pitiful calls. Had she been ordered not to do so? I lay still, waiting, for I knew some men would come soon to remove that body. Dead bodies were always removed at night or when we were all out, going around the circle.

But I did not know that the doctor, who had proven himself to be a friend to both James and me, would come first. This precious man passed so near to my hard mattress on the floor, I could have reached his hand but kept my eyes almost closed so anyone would think me sleeping. His face was very sad as he went into that little room where the body of Ila lay. I could not get up, for all our clothing was taken when we were sent to bed.

(We had to roll it into a tight roll, then it was placed in the "clothes room" behind the locked door. Then as we drew off our clothes, a huge pile of coarse, short nightgowns were there for us to put on. I was thankful that each night the pile of gowns was newly laundered. If they had not been we might have to wear one worn by someone with syphilis. There were many dying with it in hell).

When the dear doctor had gone out, walking slowly with downcast eyes, I still waited, for I knew now the men would come.

They came as I expected, almost at once, but the nurse did not make her appearance. Not once. In came the men and stretcher; they carried Ila's body out, then I arose and went to the Water Section as though for a drink.

This, to see what I knew I would find—the murderous trappings. But I found more than I thought, for in hot packs, one double woolen blanket was used with two sheets rung out of boiling water. But they had used two double, heavy woolen blankets for Ila's murder. That was a premeditated murder.

She would never torment them again; but who knows? If they had a conscience, would they never hear her pleading, "Oh, I want to go home!"? I know the attendant in charge on that July night could not bear to be there, but asked to be transferred to another ward.

Why did I not tell it? We were all forbidden to speak to doctors or visitors.

Bodies so exquisitely fashioned as was Ila's; bruised and blackened by cruel blows until the release of that spirit in hell. But then where? We know the body goes to dust except mummified by preservatives. How about the inhabitant of body, who moved out, as out of a house no longer habitable?

The large woman:

She was elderly, probably sixty or more. She bore the cruel marks of hell on body and mind, for she had suffered there a long time. She was a very large woman, weighing more than three hundred pounds, with the most enormous abdomen I ever had seen. Some kind of trouble in that region caused her continual distress. She didn't work on the ward, but I saw her coming in with the other women who worked outside the ward in one of the industries.

This woman went about crying and moaning, bringing her sad story to me, as did all those poor children.

"Oh, my poor little babies. I have carried them in my body for seven years and they can't be born. I have seven little babies inside me and they can't be born!"

Many times she repeated this mournful tale, and I suppose she did until death set her free.

A girl in her late twenties:

She would have been very pretty but was so harassed. Her body was wasting away. At the time she occupied the bed next to mine, she never slept that I knew of, for I didn't either. All day this girl worked in the laundry, all night she tried to fight off demons seen only by herself. She would lie down on her bed, but almost in a moment she would get up, grab the top sheet from her bed and pitifully beg them:

"Don't come near me! Don't come any closer! Please don't!" Then she would scream loudly.

"I'll curse you if you do, if you come any nearer!"

Then wildly flinging the sheet around her, she began to curse. Soon she would give a dreadful scream of agony as though the demon had overpowered her, and falling, would thresh around in convulsions until her body lay still. When consciousness returned, she would get up, replace the sheet on her bed, lie down, then in just moments, jumping up she would repeat the whole horrible performance.

This would go on all night, every night as long as I was in that part of the ward. What became of that poor girl I do not know. But no one could live long and suffer as she did. No one ever came near or paid any attention to her.

The young colored girl:

On this same ward, was a very attractive young colored girl slave, who worked part of the time in the "clothes room."

One day she was alone in that room, and thinking that she might call her home she took down the telephone receiver. She didn't know that she could not reach the outside on it.

There were two young southern white women attendants on duty that day. They heard her talking on the telephone for they were near. Rushing to her, they threw her to the hard floor, then taking off their sharp heeled shoes, they beat her. But feeling they could not hurt her enough with their shoes, they then removed the poor girl's heavy shoes, that all of us had to wear there, and one beat her until tired out. Then she handed the shoe to other attendant.

"Give it to her good," she said, "she's only a nigger."

How hard for me to stand there and see and hear, not being able to help that innocent girl. I never saw that girl again. To them she was "only a nigger," but she was one of God's dear children. She may have been murdered that night in a hot pack. She may have died from the cruel beating and kicking before night came.

The red-haired cripple:

Always an admirer of red hair, I could not admire this woman's hair, for although it was red in color it was as hideous as she herself. The cripple offered a moronic diversion to some of the attendants and inmates, a diversion from monotony.

The red-haired cripple! How strange and unpredictable is pride! This poor ignorant creature, crippled in body and mind, repulsive and twisted in body, was proud of the fact that the tobacco spittle from her mouth could reach a spot at least six feet away, as she stood in a circle of her admirers. No doubt some of them envied her prowess.

Scanty, carroty hair, small eyes like a pig, a large mouth in which she kept a large wad of snuff or chewing tobacco

(I think the latter). She admired herself greatly. I kept as far away from her as possible.

Her whole performance was revolting; her obscene speech, her brazen laughter and the copious onslaughts of to-bacco juice which she expectorated, thinking it was so funny when she struck someone in the face with the filthiness from her mouth. She tried the hardest to reach me, but I managed to keep just far enough away. I think she hated me.

Two of the women attendants were from her home state, and they encouraged her by listening and laughing at her. She considered herself an entertainer, dancing around the circle her listeners formed, keeping time with vulgar words from her big mouth, to the dance she called a "jig". Turning often, trying to send the filthy saliva in the direction of the one she most desired to hit. I could not even pity her, be-cause she was so diabolical.

"I am Jesus Christ!" She often cried out,

Mrs. Car and Mrs. P.:

The two who were from the cripple's home state, were the attendants who beat and kicked the young negro girl who wanted to use the telephone. They could enjoy the obscene ways of the cripple, laugh and joke with her, but they were unbelievably cruel to innocent and helpless inmates. They were dainty, lovely to look at, small, looking like high born ladies, too innocent to hurt anyone, yet I am sure there was no one in that hell more cruel than they. They loathed the helpless and hated them for no reason, but they took it upon themselves to destroy.

The little blonde school teacher:

She was also from a southern town. The attendants spoke of her on the ward, and this is her story.

She wanted to go to foreign lands as a missionary, but her parents put her into this place, to subdue her and prevent her from going.

I had no contact with her, for she was locked in a cell, she was "disturbed," they said. At night when she thought herself alone she danced, or rather pranced up and down, her heavy prison shoes which all of us were compelled to wear, making a loud noise. Her cell was so close to my bed, but I could not see or speak to her. How I pitied her! As she danced, she sang in a shrill, high voice, a not very nice song which was popular at that time. Night after night, she did this, keeping it up until she must have exhausted her strength and fallen asleep.

The lovely red-haired Irish girl:

She, too, marched and sang but not furiously. She sang, "Where the River Shannon Flows." I saw her after she was there a few days, after they freed her from her padded cell.

Her hair was a crowning glory, far below her waist, waving back from her lovely face. I often wondered if they cropped that beautiful hair and sold it. Nearly all the women who were prisoners had closely shorn hair, as that saved work, for their hair did not get any combing. If the inmates showed signs of resistance, if they rebelled the least bit, they were "disturbed."

The large, moronic girl:

She did not want to walk in line one day we were taken around the circle, saying she would not walk with us. Nothing was done to her outside where people might see, but when we went back to the ward, she was ordered into the bathroom and the door locked. There her tormentors hit, beat and at last threw her into a bathtub filled almost full with cold water. There she was held under water until she almost drowned.

The next time I saw her, days after that, she was so lame she could scarcely walk, pale, weak and silent, she walked around the circle, closely guarded by trustees.

"I thought they were going to keep me there, under that icy water, until I was dead," she told me.

She was not insane but a moron, and she feared they would kill her.

I could not go into the locked cells, but one day two young attendants took me with them.

"When we unlock this door," they said, "you go in there and bring out the night vessel."

They unlocked the door and fairly pushed me into the room, not waiting for me to enter. Quickly I felt the impact of a ferocious, demented girl. The attendants grabbed my free arm, my other hand held the vessel, and they dragged me out, locking the door behind.

In less than ten minutes they had to get help from the men attendants as they always did when something beyond their strength occurred, as often happened there. For in those few minutes the girl had torn the mattress into shreds, that strong, heavy, hard mattress! That heavy iron bed was literally torn apart, and she was using it to break down the door. She would have succeeded in a few more minutes to get out, if the attendants had not come.

The poor demented girl had no sheets, no pillows, no covers, just a bare cold mattress. She must have been given a terrible punishment, perhaps death, for I never saw or heard of her again.

So the Old Grist Mill ground them out. Some stayed a long time, some went quickly. Some were tortured for years. Some sent there sane, by their own families, to get them out of the way, then became insane under the terrible conditions there.

I knew that there was a purpose in my being there to see and hear everything God wanted me to know, in order to some day do something about it.

All of the high officers of the place called hell, although they walk through the rooms, look into all the cells, never see inside. The worst cases are drugged to keep them asleep, or they are in hot packs for their "health." None of these "patients" are permitted to tell anything of what goes on. One must be imprisoned there as a patient, whether innocent or guilty, be recognized as nothing but a "thing." Then you are treated with less consideration than that given to an animal; treated as contemptible, something low as dust, and by their count I was one of these.

They spoke of me in my presence as though I were not present, as though I were a stick of wood or piece of stone, as though I were deaf, dumb and blind. Just as they spoke of others. But I was acutely alive, my hearing, eyesight and speech were unimpaired; my mind was clear.

The suffering girl:
She used to sit on the cold iron bowl for hours every morning groaning pitifully. The water ran in those toilets all night, every night, or through them to irrigate the crops—such an irony! In the morning the water stopped. This girl was a sufferer from constipation as many were from the foods. Once a week attendants went all over the rooms, cells and everywhere, with large quantities of salts administering dosages to all alike. Great doses of salts!

I loathed all medicine, and thank God I did not need it. Strangely, they did not pour it down my throat. The only dose I ever swallowed in hell was the one the old drug addict doctor gave me. The foods were always cold when brought to us, which didn't help digestion. That large kitchen with its huge kettles must have been a sight to see! Only of course when important visitors were coming, everything was in meticulous order.

How could anyone get well under such unspeakable conditions? Human tongue cannot describe, nor human mind conceive of the horrors of hell until they have experienced it. Can I make a description adequate? Strong enough?

"No," I tell you, "I cannot."

Would you, any of you who breathe God's free air, choose to experience the damnation of hell? I did not choose it, but *one* who is *mighty* chose me in the "furnace of affliction." I am glad that *he* gave me that privilege to see and hear things that I would not have been permitted to see or hear, for they meant that I should die there and my mouth be sealed forever.

The proud lady's threats were only partially realized. She did not know the one she so cruelly hated without a cause was under the protection of the *almighty power* and *he* kept me from being a partaker with their evil deeds. Daily and at night my heart cried in pity for the thousands there without hope. Did I consider myself worthier than they? Never!

That sweet, still *voice* had said to me:

"Can I not do as I will with *my* own? Is not the gold tried in the crucible until it contains only the pure gold?"

The fact that the precious metals are tried, the precious stones are tested for reality and worth, that every natural substance is tried and proven, proves that God tries to the utmost *his* own. James and I had no other choice and knew no other God.

A young woman:

She was not named in my presence; one of the most unfortunate. Dark complexioned, slender with a perfectly formed body, she would have had a lovely face if reason had not been gone from it. Every movement was quick, graceful, reminding me of a black panther in her native haunts.

She was dressed in lovely and expensive clothing when her family came to visit her — perhaps they should have seen her as she was other times. I longed to tell them how she was beaten, kicked, starved, called every vile name by the smiling young women who led her to meet them, with their arms around her waist, calling her "darling" and "dear," smiling at her father and mother and at their unfortunate young daughter. She was probably eighteen years old but may have been a little younger. They brought many nice gifts for her, especially foods and candies, none of which passed her lips.

"She has just had her lunch," they were told.

The smiling hypocrites looked as if they adored the child, but she was kept locked in a padded cell almost all the time. When I carried trays to the bed patients, this girl, when not locked up, stole the food from the trays because she was starving. Then I had to get the nurse to put more food on the trays.

"Don't let her steal the food any more," they told me.

But it was impossible to prevent all the time. I would much rather have given her a whole tray of food.

One day I saw her searching the laundry, which had been carried out and left in the hall. All at once she gave a cry like a wild animal (she never spoke a word in my hearing, just uttered coarse, guttural cries), grabbed a menstrual cloth, clotted and vile, and putting it to her mouth, greedily ate the contents, then searched for more.

Did I tell the nurses? No, they would have said, "Your crazy mind made it up." I found it nothing but the *power* of God that could change the leper's spots, not speaking of the poor girl as a leper but of the people who ruled in hell.

I saw women drinking their own urine.

"I can't get any water to drink and this is good and cold," one poor old woman told me. What I don't need to drink I pour on my head, for my head is so hot."

This was so terrible!

But no one cared, of the attendants who were supposed to wait on such people, they simply ignored it. Of the patients who were sane enough and sorry enough, not one could get behind those locked doors to give a drink of water to the suffering creatures. If they could see them, it was only through that small aperture in that heavy locked door. There were bars on that small hole, and it was impossible to pass one of the drinking bowls through that opening.

I can still see that poor old, bald, gray colored head, which the woman said was so hot. Oh, the pity of it! The helplessness of my strength! This hole in the door was the only ventilation for the cells, as there were no windows, even when the temperature was 104 degrees, or more.

"These people are here for us to cure them," those in charge said when speaking of the sick.

It was unbelievable, for in all the time spent by me there, I saw them try to make just two people well. One of them, the young girl who was beaten unconscious by Mary A. The other was Kate, who had pneumonia. When the parents of the young girl, who was beaten, came to visit her they were told she had rheumatism. Her body, hands and head were swathed in woolen blankets to hide her wounds.

Kate had no parents, no visitors, but she was an extremely good slave. She was large and strong, "tough as iron" as
people say; but when she took ill she almost died.

"Oh, let me die! Let me die!" she begged continually.

But they nursed her day and night, doing everything they
could to help her, and she recovered.

Years after that I saw Kate in the home of a very wealthy
family where she worked as a domestic. To my horror, Kate
was in the bedroom of a young woman of the family, giving
her a massage. I wondered how she came to be employed
there, for Kate, in those other days, had been at times very
violent and difficult to subdue. Surely this elderly, wealthy
society lady would not accept domestic help blindly!

One day into this lowest hell, came the proud one with a
lady officer of the prison to see how people were cared for, I
suppose. This visitor was a beautiful woman in her thirties,
an air of sweetness and breeding showed in her face and her
manner. As my enemy passed me I spoke to her.

"Oh, how could you send me to this horrible place?"

My only complaint while there.

She made no reply, but to the question on that visitor's
sweet face, she answered:

"This is one of our puerperal patients."

She went on talking as they moved away, and by her
manner I knew she was informing the lady, who had been
sorry for me, of all my horrible deeds.

Time passed as it must, even in hell, and August came.
It was very lovely outside, and extremely hot and fetid
inside. Hot outside too, but the breeze was cooling.

My three arch enemies, the superintendent, the red-
haired doctor, the proud lady and perhaps many more went
on vacation that month. As soon as they left, the kind and

humane doctor friend, told me he was sending me to Cottage __, supposed to be the "best" place in hell.

So the last day I awakened in that first lowest hell, and after breakfast, took the syphilitic girl, into whose bed I was put on my arrival on that ward, to the Receiving Cottage for her treatment, as usual. Everyday, as I had been escorting her, I could stand at the door of the treatment room and see my beloved Bible inside. Whether the proud lady put it there to tempt me or to taunt me I didn't know, but never did I touch it, much as I wanted to.

But on this last day, no one objected when I resolutely walked into the treatment room and took this most precious thing I could see in the dark place...my Bible. I knew if I didn't take it then, I might not have another opportunity.

In hell they often said, "There is no time here." It was
an eternity of suffering.

Part IV
BEST COTTAGE

THE NEW LIBERTY BELL

Once we looked to a thing of steel,
That rang in the long ago,
A poor old bell, with a rended side;
But today we look to a *voice* that is real,
And will set this world aglow.

He too, had a rended side,
Because *he* is the *one who* died,
Who died, but now is risen,
The *voice* of God, the *new* and *living bell*,
To rescue souls from hell.

This *bell* is now made whole,
And *it's* sound shall ring through all the earth,
Redeemed shall be each soul,
Through that glad new *birth*!

Of flesh? Nay, but of the *spirit's power*,
He *who* raised up Christ,
Shall raise you in that hour,
That hour of *life* anew, for all
Who sacrificed their life, for *him who* died.

BEST COTTAGE

My first meal at the *Best Cottage*, was a startling experience. The table was set with a white cloth, freshly ironed, silverware of a kind, dishes of sturdy ware, and not the tin plates and large tin spoons of the lower wards.

I learned our mealtimes were the same early hours, morning, mid day and afternoon. Never noon and never night. We had to be in bed at 4:30 P.M., and be up at 4:30 A.M. So at 11:30 A.M., that first day, I walked from the hall into this delightful (compared to the others) looking dining room. A nice, pleasant looking woman served our table, occupied by three other women and myself. I seated myself at the south end of the table, which was my place while there.

Something beyond myself caused me to lift my plate carefully upward from the table's edge. What I saw was most shocking, but I made no sound. There was a napkin under that plate, dry, but literally stiff with red blood! Every fiber of that napkin had been steeped in fresh blood.

Why? To frighten me? To see how controlled I could be? I never learned anything about it.

Quietly laying the plate down just as it had been, and keeping the plate as a shield so none of the others could see the napkin, I beckoned the serving woman to me. Carefully I lifted the plate so she alone could see the napkin.

"I'll bring you another plate," she said without a shudder.

She took the plate and napkin away, and returned with a clean looking plate and freshly ironed white napkin.

"Thank you," I said.

This attendant may have been completely innocent of knowing what was under my plate, or she may have been ordered to place it there. I never knew which.

The food looked clean for the potatoes were boiled plain, but peeled before cooking. There was skimmed milk to drink instead of water. Afterward I watched the women washing and drying those clean looking dishes as they worked. They seemed utterly unconscious of it. So, each meal I took my napkin and scrubbed my dishes as hard as I could, knowing it was not enough. Still one had to eat something, and I could not leave my place to wash dishes. It was just one of the "minor" things of hell.

Those long August days in the cottage, I did the same things I had done at the first two places. But besides the usual routine, Caro, with whom I was re-united, and I were given the work by the head nurse of taking care of the dining room, setting tables, counting silver, and other tasks which she complimented us on doing so well. Why not? We liked to work and knew how.

I could look across a long, wide space and see James outside working, or at the third story window of the ward he was in, sitting close by the window, always with his beloved Bible. I was not near enough to speak, or to have him speak to me, but we had a language no one else knew. We could understand each other and know what was going on without words.

For that one month I had my Bible, then it was taken away until my debt was paid to man's law. Caro and I read after we were compelled to go to bed at 4:30 P.M., each day. We could not go out and walk among the lovely trees and flowers, as we could see the nurses and attendants walking side by side. Their gay laughter, seeming such a mockery in that dreaded hell, was brought to us through the locked and barred doors and windows.

Flowers of every hue, blooming in beautiful profusion, shrubs with their sweet perfume, and the perfume of thousands of roses of different colors. Birds, bees and butterflies flying; birds singing; butterflies with their rainbow hued beauty seeking a place to hide their eggs under some leafy plant, so the enemies, such as birds and destructive insects would not find their young to destroy them. Birds flitted from tree to tree and sang their grateful thanks to God for *his* loving care.

He said, *"Behold the birds of the air, they sow not neither do they reap, nor gather into barns, yet your heavenly father feedeth them. Are ye not much better than they?"* Matthew 6:26.

Butterflies flitted back and forth, lovely as flowers, believing their little ones safe from spiders. And they were so near to the place of torment, utterly unconscious of it. The many hives of bees were busy making honey, carrying loads of sweetness. They, too, sang their song of grateful thanks to our *maker*.

"Everything worships God but man," it is written.

My bed at the Best Cottage was near the window, which was raised, and only the bars kept us from seeing more fully. The breeze at this place brought the birds' song, the bees' song and the flitting beauty of the butterflies we could see. The birds we could also see, but the bees we could hear. The other unfortunates in this cottage, were, with the exception of Caro, too low in their mentality to seem to realize their condition. They laughed, made coarse, unlovely jokes, sang and talked, not caring because they could not feel the awfulness of hell. Nearly all of them had passed under the knife and were soon to be sent out on probation, a few to go back to their homes. Those flowers we saw, we could not touch; those birds, we could not feed; the honey made from the blossoms, we never tasted.

I did not covet those things.

Now that my Lord assured me that our death in that place was not to be a physical death, I longed for freedom for James and myself, that we might go to our little son and join the few of that little band who believed in us and in the great *name* of Jesus Christ, which we had manifested to them according to the *revelation* of the *scriptures*. But I did not know that I would again be placed in one of the lowest hells. Acutely alive to everything around me, acutely longing, now at last, for that precious liberty to again preach the *truth* and much more comprehensively.

While in this cottage, my friends had brought me a blank book in which I wrote out the *revelation* given me years before of the *father's name*, the *scriptures* testifying of it, and the promise of a son to be born to me. One morning the good doctor came and said that he wanted to talk to me.

At his questioning, I told him all that had occurred, of how James and I had preached together; had starved, almost, together; had made our marriage vows before our friends, kneeling in humbleness; about the promise of a son the year before as we sat on a hillside with our Bibles; of God's promise to me the same year he *revealed his name* to me, of a *son* to be born to me; and told me to call *his name* Jesus. Of our love for God, but no desire to commit sin or to break the law, which we knew we had been compelled to break. I told him of the signs following my son's conception; of the *heavenly* music a few hours before his birth; and how Mercy heard and said, "It is not earthly music." Of how she told me of the "halos" around his head and mine, always, when he was in my longing arms at night, tenderly placed there by her gentle hands.

The doctor listened earnestly, quietly, to every word.

"Well, I can't judge," he said. "I don't know God's plan; I am on the outside. But as long as you differ from the world, they will adjudge you to be insane."

Did God put these wonderful words into his mouth to comfort me? And the words he spoke to a nurse who was my friend.

"I am never in her (calling me by name) presence, but what she makes me feel like a better man."

How comforting that was to me, those kind words from such a kind man, who was never unkind to anyone there, and who made things better for them if he could.

When the doctor left my presence that day, I gave him all the things I had written of the *scriptures* and songs. He kept them a few days, then returned them to me, saying they were "good."

I did not know that in a few days, as soon as the "terrible three" returned from vacation, I would be sent back to one of the lowest hells. There to suffer many things I had experienced before, and any hope of release grew far remote. For September brought me to the place where I had to refuse to obey the laws or rules of hell to obey the *law* of God. All that hard work imposed on me in those long months, had been done without a murmur or question. It would have been so much easier to work than to refuse, not from fear of them, but because the time passed better when I worked and when I waited on the sick and suffering ones.

Then the red-haired woman doctor came back from her vacation. She was not pleased that the kind doctor had transferred me from the first lowest hell, to which the proud lady had assigned me before going on their vacations.

The women of one particular ward were out for their little walk around the circle, and were resting on the ground for the allotted five minutes, when the red-haired doctor drove past in her new blood-red car. In one surge they rose from the ground to their feet, but not to do honor to the doctor. Their gaunt arms were raised high above their heads.

"Blood! Blood!" they screamed. "Her car is covered with blood!"

Was it not true? Many of them had that long, ugly scar. Their blood had been shed. They had been to slaughter, taken unaware, not knowing what would be done to them.

In hell they often said, "There is no time here." No, it was an eternity of suffering, of being goaded with opprobrious insulting remarks heaped upon my head, through all of which I made no complaint. It was a place where I suffered for the touch of baby fingers, of sweet baby lips; for kind and comforting words; for loved voices of friends; even for food, clean, wholesome food. When I arose in the morning I was hungry, and went to bed hungry every afternoon.

The last day of August I was assigned to work on a machine in the sewing room. My kimonos were by this time nothing more than rags, so now that I was under the good doctor's supervision, dresses were made for me like the other inmates wore. But mine, being new, were not faded as most of theirs were.

Two dresses and a pair of shoes I received for my wages in hell. Cotton dresses; one gray, one a kind of blue. The shoes were plain and common. I had not asked for anything, and having no money I could not buy a new "wardrobe." I would not send for my meager belongings left behind that morning that seemed ages ago, in the place where James and I made our home for a little while.

My home! Once, before being called by the *name* of the Lord, I had a lovely home and friends. But they were friends no more and that home was gone forever.

Alice:

She had been at the Receiving Cottage when I had first been taken there. Alice, a small, slender young woman who spent the daytime hours in the sewing room. Alice, who was promised that she could go home after they cut out her "kimono," as the keepers mockingly and laughingly called the operation of sterilization. They operated little, gentle Alice some time during those terrible six weeks that I was in bed after my son's birth. Then she was sent here, to the Best Cottage after her recovery.

"Alice," I exclaimed when I saw her in the sewing room, "I thought you had gone home long ago!"

Alice could not hold up her pretty head. She was so thin and weak, that she had to lean her head on the sewing machine as she sewed.

"No, I did not go home. They did not keep their word."

Alice would never go home, only to the place God had prepared for her. Her tired body might go home in a casket, but the life of that body would be gone.

Liars cannot enter the heaven God has prepared for *his* people; but they are not barred from hell. Little Alice was a dove. How long did Alice live? I do not know, for this was my only day in the sewing room.

Our forelady told about twelve of us that she was going to give us some lunch. It was to be brought down on the elevator from the kitchen where the staff of doctors, nurses and attendants had their food prepared.

"Do not tell anyone about this," she cautioned us.

She often did this for her help, but I had not been there before so it was my first time to know about it. Expecting nice, clean food for the first time in nine months, how I would enjoy it, I thought.

Down came the elevator with real coffee, with cream and sugar in it; luscious beefsteak, cold but tender and good. But the coffee was hot! Each of us was served by the kind lady who appreciated our work in the sewing room.

I had just taken my first bite of that delicious beefsteak and a sip of coffee, when into the midst of our feasting stepped the immaculate superintendent back from vacation.

"What does this mean?" he cried sharply to our kind forelady. "Take this food away at once and don't ever do such a thing again!"

He, it seemed, would rather have that good food poured out to the hogs than given to unpaid, hungry, hard working women. All of us had just begun to eat. I accepted the loss of the food calmly, silently, but some complained bitterly, some almost cried.

"What shall I do now?" one elderly woman wailed. "The coffee kept me regular, and now I must suffer."

It was in the early morning hours of that same night, the first day of September, that my blessed Lord commanded me in *his* sweet still *voice*.

"Labor not for the meat that perisheth, but for that meat which the son of man shall give unto you, for him hath God the father sealed." John 6:27.

I knew what *he* meant and no matter what it cost, I knew that I had to obey. And in the morning at the call to go to the sewing room, I refused to go.

"No," I said, "I will not work here any more."

But my refusal was not accepted quietly. I was ordered to, told that I should be compelled to go to work. The matron of the cottage even came and urged me to go.

"No," I also told her, "I am not going to work here any more."

Then the head of the sewing department came. I had written a letter of explanation to the superintendent which I gave to her, asking if she would give it to him. She replied that she would.

"I have given the superintendent my reasons for not going to work."

The next morning this sewing department head again came to tell me to go to work.

"You must go to work!" she commanded.

"No, I won't." Then I asked, "Did you give the superintendent my letter?"

"No, he is too busy a man to be bothered with your delusions."

"Very well, I will write it again."

She left me. I wrote the letter over, and in just a few minutes we were taken out to go around the circle. There I met the superintendent face to face. I had been forbidden to speak to a doctor or anyone without permission, but I gave the letter into his own hand, and he read it while I stood there. Another thing I was not supposed to do was to stop or step out of line, but this day no one said or did anything to me.

Having read the letter, the superintendent made one comment to which I answered. Then he walked on his way and I went with the others to walk around the circle and sit on the ground.

The next morning, September third, I was sent to the second lowest hell.

The horrible meals were served in the basement. The foods were cooked in great iron kettles by "patients," men who no doubt were insane, for nothing was clean. A large scoop was used to scoop the food from the kettles, together with strings, gravel, worms, bugs, and dirt. Most patients were emaciated, starving, exhausted from slaving in the many industries and work asssignments they were forced to do.

Part V
SECOND LOWEST HELL

THE CROSS IN HELL

Three days in hell, three days among the damned,
Embowelled in the earth, "They gaped upon me with their mouth,"
The flames of fire around the cross had no power to burn,
Nor leave the smell of fire upon *his* garments.
"A sword shall pierce through thine own heart,
That the thoughts of many hearts may be *revealed*,"
Was truly said, and one was there with broken heart,
Cast alive into the fire, *who*, on *his* right hand stood,
And one was there with blackened heart, who, on *his* left
    side stood,
The cross had *power* even there to comfort broken hearts.

How the rabble mocked and spat upon that *holy child*,
Nor water gave to quench *his* thirst,
Nor meat *his* hunger gave to satisfy,
Nor in *his* sickness did they visit *him*,
Nor in *his* prison came to cheer;
But those three days in hell,
God's glory shone 'round that cross e'en there,
And there was wrought through *his* own *son* perfection.
Three days to build that temple strong,

Nor rains nor floods have power to move,
And e'en in hell the cross o'ershadowed was by God's great *love*.

For deep in earth it is that seeds do grow,
And from the earth spring forth,
"Except a corn of wheat fall into the ground and die,"
Alone it abideth.
But if it die, much fruit it bringeth forth.
From out of the earth the cross springs forth,
The corn of wheat is risen,
And life will give to all good seed,
And death is overcome through life.

The cross that from the darkness sprung,
Of ages gone before, now shines with glorious light.
The sign of Jonah is fulfilled.
No other sign shall sinners see.
"It is finished," from the cross was spoken,
And who can hinder what God has planned?
The gulf is bridged, death's river crossed,
The dove has found a place to rest her feet,
Death overcomes, hell o'ercome, grave overcome!
"Oh death! Where is thy sting?"

Israel's *deliverer*, yes, and *king* is *he*!
And now shall come a ransomed host,
In the *name* of the *father, son* and *holy ghost*.

The resurrection *bower* came through those three days in hell,
And the fullness of *life* came through Jesus Christ,
Who is the *father, son* and *holy ghost*,
And none can usurp *his* authority,
Nor can they *his holy name* deny,
Jesus Christ, the same yesterday and today and forever.

Second Lowest Hell

At the second lowest hell, all my writings were confiscated the first day, (although later given back). Taking me on my entrance into a padded cell, a tall lady confronted me.

"Now we want you to give up your things," she demanded.

I reached into my pocket and surrendered them without a word. She had taken me into that padded cell so that if I made any resistance she could do with me as she wished, and no one could pass that locked door or interfere with her. I was not afraid, but had learned enough about how hot packs and other awful punishments were administered to ever think of resisting. If I had been insane, I would have resisted, for I would not have known the consequences to follow.

"We hate to take your Bible and things from you," she lied.

But I thought to myself, "Even if they take every material thing away I have in my possession, they cannot take away what God has given into my mind."

So, taking my Bible and the things God had caused me to write, and my pencil Mercy had given me, she unlocked the door and motioned to me to sit down on a long bench opposite another identical one. On either side of me were insane women, opposite me insane women. I could not walk away. There was only the length of the hall and barred doors locked at each end of that hall.

The only other place to go was the Water Section, a malodorous place no sane person would linger in. The toilet
bowls in there were cold, hard, unpainted iron. No seat, no
covering for the bowls, and scarcely ever any paper, unless
you asked for it. Then sometimes, though not always, you
were given it by the attendant. Often they said, "There is
none." These seats of iron were so cold in winter, but not
colder than the hearts of them who ruled there.

In the second lowest hell, they tried to get me to work but
I would not.

"Do you think yourself better than the others?" one
woman taunted me after I refused to work. "If you were better than they you would not be here."

How I longed to open those darkened, distorted minds!
To set the pitiful "captives free!"

But they grew to love me on this last ward.

"We don't know how we'll get along without you," some
of the nurses said.

I was treated more kindly here than on the others, but the
same awful ways prevailed as in the others. The same horrors were perpetrated.

Only the women who were in hell for drink habit or some
light offense could have access to matches or stores, like
hundreds there were guilty of, but not called insane. Sometimes these women were sent to the diet kitchen to prepare
food at night. This was not permitted by daylight. One day
the head of the ward came to me as I sat on a long bench in
the hall with nothing to do but look at dreary, idiotic faces in
front of me and on both sides of me.

"Oh," this young woman said, "I've just got to confide in
someone, I'm so worried. One of the patients was knocked
down and beaten on the basement floor this morning. It is
almost noon and she is still unconscious."

"Have you called a doctor?" I asked.

"No, I'm afraid to call a doctor."

"But she may die."

"All right, I will get a doctor."

But the woman died.

It was a control I exercised over myself all the time I was in hell, not to ask questions. If I had, I might have been told who destroyed the life of that quiet, hardworking woman on the cement floor of the basement that day. For the one who confided in me loved me and often asked me of the things of God.

The general rule followed there was, "You're insane. Why are you concerned with others?" So I was very quiet and calm, seeing everything I was meant to see, and knowing many things I was not supposed by them to know, as those in charge were secretive as a rule.

My dear friend, I now want you and all the world to know about the foods we were compelled to eat in hell.

The first time I ate in the second hell is almost indescribable. We had been sitting on long benches, each long enough to seat about twenty people. These seats were placed on either side of the hall. This was the same in all the wards on all those long hall floors, except the Receiving Cottage.

The people here were worse off than the people at the Receiving Cottage. These had been passed through the "mill"; they were for the most part hopeless cases incarcerated for life.

I had gone through the routine of bath and hair washing which I had experienced before being brought there that morning, but the rule must be obeyed. There was no walking about the circle that day, but soon being called to dinner at 11:30 A.M., we went into the basement. A large basement, with dirt walls and cement floors identical with others I saw there.

This basement had other occupants besides helpless people; it was tenanted by rats, mice and cats. The cats had boxes half filled with dirt, but they were so seldom emptied that the odors were terrible and mingled with the odors of rodents, which made it even worse. The odors of diseased, unclean bodies, were no help to keen nostrils like mine either, for my nature loved cleanliness, sweetness, perfumes of nature; and I abhorred the smells and sights of hell. There was no way to escape bad odors in hell; just endure until the break came. But they could not break my mind.

In the basement we sat at the long tables on long benches like those in the halls. But no sooner had some of those poor lost souls sat down than one was seized with an epileptic attack, which I had never seen before. I started to rise to see if I could help her, but was quickly reprimanded.

"Keep your hands off of her," an attendant said sharply. "We never touch them; just let them alone."

The victim had fallen backward to that hard cement floor with a shrill scream. Out of her mouth poured bloody foam, her body was convulsed into a grotesque shape, her limbs were flailing the hard cement.

But that was not all! Quickly from both sides of the table others fell, each emitting the same heart breaking screams until five were on the floor. This was horrible to see and hear. I had seen much before my little son was born, but I was glad to be spared this until now. After awhile these epileptics lay still as if dead for sometime, then got up and sat down; but there was no dinner for them that day and none for me. How could one eat under these conditions? There was a repetition of this almost every day, and I learned to turn my eyes away and not to hear, for I was starving there.

The foods were cooked in great iron kettles by "patients," men who no doubt were insane, for nothing was clean. A large scoop was used to scoop the food from the kettles, together with strings, gravel, worms, bugs, and dirt. Lumps of it!

One day it was cabbage and small, very small potatoes. These were about the size of black walnuts and as black; some even smaller than walnuts. The patients ate them with the black coating of earth and the skins; but when I was able to get any, I peeled them. This meal, together with two slices of dark bread, served without butter or any spread, no dessert, and only water to drink, was served on alternate days for both dinner and supper.

Always on the day following the cabbage and potato day, the foods were beans and "stew" which was made of infinitesimal pieces of unidentifiable sinews of some kind of meat. This was mixed with flour and cooked just into a doughy consistency, with tiny bits of carrots and potatoes. That was the stew! Thus the dinner and supper meals alternated each day with the two meals of cabbage and potatoes, then the two meals of beans and stew.

James and I compared our knowledge of foods there, afterwards when we were free, and found that we both had to contend with the rocks, the sticks, the worms, the bugs and the string. There was never any gravy or soup, because I think it would have been thrown in the faces of opposite unfortunates at the same table. Water thrown did not make so much muss.

We were never served raw vegetables at any time, no melons, no fruit at breakfast, except prunes, watery, wormy prunes. If these prunes had ever had juice, it had been extracted. And weevils and worms floated on the top of them.

Do you, any of you, think this is an exaggeration? If you do, go there under the guise of a helpless patient.

Also for breakfast, besides the prunes, was served the inevitable two slices of dark bread, probably dark from dirty hands that mixed it, and no spread for that bread. A small dish of half cooked oatmeal, a little bluish milk on it, but no sugar ever for anything. At this meal we had something they called coffee to drink, but that smelled to me like steel filings smell. One cup of that was all they gave us. And that was breakfast every day, seven days each week, month after month, and year after year.

No change, no enticing odors of good foods. These three menus were served monotonously day after day.

You who have never been partakers of such as this—I mean all of you everywhere who are privileged to eat clean, wholesome foods, you may reflect on your fellow human beings. But if you think of it and never try to alleviate it, you may not always enjoy your delicious foods, spread so abundantly before you, of which you may partake in quiet leisure. We had fifteen minutes from the time we sat down until we were herded away to go to work or to bed.

You who do not understand, may say, "Well, they deserved it; they brought it on themselves. I don't care if they suffer."

Who is the judge?

One said long ago, "*Let him who is without sin among you first cast a stone.*" John 8:7.

But Cain asked, "*Am I my brother's keeper?*" Genesis 4:9.

Remember, Cain was a murderer. There are many "keepers" in hell who are murderers.

If you will not eat that food, or cannot eat it, the attendants will call enough of their "trustees" to hold you and forcibly feed you that horrible looking, slimy mixture in a rubber container with a long tube attachment. This tube which is forced up one nostril, bringing blood, until it reaches the throat and the mixture is poured into it and down the throat. This is repeated until the unfortunate eats again or never eats, for death intervenes sometimes under cruel pressure.

At the Receiving Cottage and other cottages, foods looked clean but were of poor quality. We had the same prunes, oatmeal and coffee, cooked in the same manner, the same blue milk, no butter or spread for breakfast, the same number of slices of dark bread. But the other two meals looked clean and vegetables varied from day to day. No salad, no fruit, either cooked or uncooked ever. They served milk for dinner and supper, skimmed milk of course.

There were white table cloths and napkins on some of the tables. There was tableware, which was counted before and after meals, for protection of attendants, nurses and favorites; others did not matter. It was a relief to the authorities to get inmates out of the way if they were hated. A knife or fork, even a large spoon, would make a formidable weapon in the hands of a maniac.

On the wards, foods were placed at intervals down the center of bare, rough tables. The foods were in old graniteware bowls and there was never half enough, for the people worked hard and were hungry. Sometimes and often, one would grab a dish and empty its contents on her plate. There were fights in the basement over the food, at which I looked on fearfully or called the attendants if the fighting got too hard.

After putting the foods on the table or having patients do the work for them, the ladies always left the room except on a few occasions. I guess they couldn't stand the sight and smells. The thousands of people went through this continually, but the staff of doctors, nurses and attendants had the best foods cooked by cooks of sound minds; each cottage or ward had a diet kitchen where foods were prepared. The favored bed patients were fed good food from those kitchens. This I know too, for I carried trays and fed them. I did not envy them their foods for there was never enough for them, poor things, and why should I have better foods than the others who worked hard day and night too?

With all the bountiful crops of fruits and vegetables of every kind at that place, it was incredible that we were never given any of them. There were great fields of potatoes, corn, beans green and lovely, peas, vegetables of every kind in great abundance, and all kinds of fruits. Oranges, lemons, grapefruit, peaches, and olive orchards, pomegranates, too many to mention.

But none for us.

I used to see men attendants bringing large amounts of luscious fruit to the ladies of the place, the ladies who looked on while the slaves did the work they were paid to do.

There was a large dairy; there were herds of cattle for meat, some sheep and many hogs. We had none of that meat. There was butter made daily, none for us. There was an ice factory, electric plants, shoe factory, mattress factory, laundries, all kinds of industries kept up by the work of slaves.

There was a sewing shop, it was very large and equipped with many machines, for all the clothing worn by the people under authority of the jailers, was made there by those peoples' hands. All the sheets, pillow cases, night wear, dresses, aprons, overalls and jackets were made all in the same fashion. Some were very large, some were small. The plain dresses were of two colors, either plain grey or plain blue. The shoes made in the factory were heavy, with thick soles and heels.

There was a dentist's place. But was the man who did the work a real dentist? I was thankful I did not have to see him, for reports by sufferers at his rough hands were enough for me to know he was heartless.

The authorities must have shipped away much of the abundant supplies there, which were supposed to be fed to the "patents," but we were starving and received not.

Poor, who have been compelled to accept county aid, have thought their lot hard; the humiliation of the treatment they have received bitter; but if they could compare their lot with the people in hell, they would thank God; for they can walk or ride, they can sleep, the can have their families with them and if they do not have just the best, they are not starved, not all of them.

The cabbage I used to cut from my garden would crackle with freshness; the cabbage in hell could be identified only by the odor. The beans I cooked in my home made my mouth water by their fragrance; those in hell had too much dirt, pieces of manila rope, stones and worms. I was hungry all through the long days, weeks and months of my stay, only when too ill or sorrow filled even to care or think of eating. I never rushed to pick up a dish, or strove to get food before others had served themselves. No one could blame you for not eating if you could get nothing to eat; but if you did without eating deliberately, woe be unto you!

When the attendants and the nurses had "purloined goodies" for a party, I did not envy them, nor covet the good food. Why should I be better fed than the thousands of unfortunate people there and in many such places, dying, starving, suffering, some in strait jackets, tied to beds hand and foot. I knew that I was blessed above those suffering ones, for I had been given a sound mind, a mind that could never become mentally ill, a mind that could never be changed, only as the great God would change it. He who had given me that mind to obey and worship *him*.

My "daily bread" was supplied by *his spirit*, bringing into my mind *his* blessed *words*. Though hungry for nourishing food, clean food, no one ever heard me say so. Hungry too, for loved ones, hungry for sunshine and fresh, clean air.

Many were sent out of hell on "probation" and the "dumb ones" as they were called, were robbed of their wages by the probationers. One day the proud lady sent word for me to go to her office, and an attendant took me there. The proud one introduced me to an elderly, hard faced woman.

"This is my probation officer," she said.

"Do you want me to handle your case?" the woman asked.

My answer was quick and decisive.

"No, I want you to have absolutely nothing to do with my case."

Then immediately I was taken back to the lowest hell. I wanted freedom, not probation; spying on my every action and a return to that place on some trumped up lie, if my every action did not please the spies and their masters. Many were returned in that way and became prey to melancholy and despair. I met some of them there who had been returned.

Speaking of visitors, when they left the wards leaving nice foods and gifts for their loved ones, candies, cakes, fried chicken or anything they knew would be enjoyed by their child, wife, husband, mother, father or friend, as the case might be; the visitors must place these presents in the hands of the attendants to give to the patients. Usually this was the rule, but occasionally, miraculously, as with my box of candy, they were given into the hands of them for whom they were intended. The recipients did not taste them, however, for as soon as the relative or friend left, an attendant said:

"Now give us these things and we will put them away for you until you are hungry."

"I'm hungry now!" the victim would always protest.

I never saw anyone there who was not hungry, only the dying ones and the recent operative cases. The inmates never saw that food again, but soon the attendants would have a party and the "goodies" would be served to the other attendants who were their friends. Two of them invited me to one of their feasts one night.

"If you will bring one of the bowls from the water section," they said, "we will give you some of our supper."

"No thank you," I replied.

I could not tell them what I had seen women do with those same bowls, for I saw them squatted over the bowls, washing their most intimate parts. The poor souls were bathed once a week, but were not to have any personal cleanliness at any other time. The bathrooms were always locked; they were given no wash basins, and there were no stationary washbowls.

The women drank from those bowls day and night, but never did I drink from them, other than my first night in hell. I drank water from the faucets, not letting my mouth touch them. These young women attendants called nurses, but many of them could not even read a thermometer and knew nothing of nursing, would not have believed me, or would they? They could have seen as I did, these things being done. Could I blame those poor, starved, beaten, kicked, mind-sick children for trying to be clean? No, I sorely pitied them.

The bathing was done once a week. The routine at the Receiving Cottage had been:

Each one was taken into a bathroom, put into a tub containing a few inches of tepid water, given two minutes in that tub, washed by an attendant, not permitted to bathe themselves, taken out and given a clean bundle of coarse, faded garments to put on. Between eighty-five and one hundred were bathed in the space of a few hours, allotting two minutes to each bath. The tubs were not even rinsed out with cold water, just emptied and three or four inches of water run into them from the faucet. Sometimes no more than two inches of water.

Another day of the week was hair washing. This was also done in the bathroom in grimy tubs with strong fish oil soap. Imagine how your hair would feel, look and smell. Then the hair combing followed. Everyone was combed with a "common" comb, the same comb on sore, diseased scalps, hideous scalps. But what could we do about it? The first time this happened to me I objected.

"I brought my own comb. I like individual cleanliness."

"Do you think yourself better than the others?"

"No," I answered, but my flesh shrank from the contact of such a comb.

Some of the women had vermin in their hair and their heads were treated, after washing, to kill the vermin. But how could one be sure that they were exempt after having such a comb used on their head? But that was a minor horror of hell.

The fish oil soap left our bodies coated with an ill-smelling scum, our hair the same, and by the time for another weekly bath the odor was just beginning to wear away. This was renewed by the next ordeal. So by this replenishing, we were never free from that odor. If one was moved to another ward, and had just had a bath, it did not matter; the operation was gone through at the next place just as though it would make us clean. I know this was done, for I experienced it.

In the other wards, including this second lowest hell, but the cottages not included, the women were all ordered and brought into a large bathroom having a number of tubs. That is, all were brought but bed patients or those in strait jackets. Then they were stripped nude, if they did not know enough to strip themselves. When I saw the sheets spread out on the floor, for the first time, I wondered why that was done.

I did not have long to wonder.

A great pile of coarse, faded garments and a heap of towels were piled at one side of the room. For that pile I took a towel and draped it around my body, for though I were in hell, numbered with the damned, I could not give up to that state of beasts, since I had been "cast alive into the fire." But to see a hundred or more women, pinched faces out of which all hope had fled; gaunt, hunger-wasted and disease-wasted bodies, used day and night as slaves; shaven heads; long abdominal scars running almost the full length of tortured bodies; was to me a horrible and hideous sight. Some of these bodies were covered with festering sores; some were marked with deep scars from hot-pack cruelties, some were deformed.

The first day in the second lowest hell, when I had been taken from the Best Cottage, as we were in the bathroom, naked for all who came in to behold us, into the doorway stepped the beautiful, proud lady. This lovely and poised lady had the audacity to make this observation.

"How wonderful!" she said, smiling at the scene.

And I answered her explosively.

"How horrible!"

Like cattle at a watering place these poor creatures left their droppings, and one must be careful where they stepped.

Then I understood the need of the sheets.

Some of those same creatures toiled each day in the laundry room to wash those same sheets, as well as all the other coarse, faded garments; washed in that strong, yellow, evil smelling soap.

Not one of those unfortunate ones spoke a word all the time they were in that room. They had learned, through bitter punishment, to keep silent. But God had opened my eyes and my mouth and I had no fear of them, for death would have been sweet to me that day. I had scars, too; scars inside my being, scars of loneliness and sorrow.

The air was foul, no adjective could describe it.

"This air is so thick you could cut it with a knife," some of the lady attendants said.

On occasions, some of the unfortunates cursed it, as men curse. There they stood, a pack of slaves, denuded of every earthly thing, even the greatest of all—motherhood. I had *one* to heal my scars, my *merciful* and *just one*, Jesus Christ; but they; if ever they had a hope of justice, it had been taken from them. They were bruised and naked and left to die. While I knew that I had a savior to heal my wounded soul, I knew they had no one. I was forbidden to speak His *name* there, but I did on every occasion that was presented me. My heart cried out for them standing there. I cried to God for them.

On bath days I always took my wash rag from the room and used it in the Water Section after each irony of a thing they called a bath. I washed my face and hands with clean, cold water, but those poor ones did not dare to do that. I was not supposed to, but knew that I could take that privilege; it was only human to do so.

The dentists "pulled" teeth from the people in hell, but made them no dentures. They could not bite if their teeth were out. Some probably lost their teeth because of biting attendants.

No scissors, no hairpins, nor any kind of pin was allowed to the people there. No mirrors hung on the walls to reflect one's image. Finger nails were cut short; no pencils, no newspapers, no books, no Bibles, no stationary. Everything was taken away. Even when sitting on the ground after going around the circle, if one took up any stone, even a small one, or stick, it was quickly taken away. The inmates could look but not touch anything.

The greater number chewed their fingernails, but some tried to keep them, to let them grow long—claws to scratch with. They were so angry when their fingernails were cut almost to the quick. How anyone could chew their fingernails was so repulsive to me, but then many revolting things were done in hell.

Many ate and drank emanations from their own bodies. And some ate repulsive clots from menstrual cloths. I never spoke of these things to the attendants, for they would have said, "You are crazy," or, "It is a lie." But the Bible bears witness to every horrible thing that is committed in that hell and undoubtedly all the others. It was easy for the attendants to ignore such things when they saw them, for they did not have to be locked behind iron bars with them. They did not have to eat with them nor sleep just twelve inches from them. Perhaps they knew, perhaps they knew also of the hideous and unlawful practices of the depraved ones with each other in the darkness of night and in their darkened minds.

Those shorn heads! Some of them were bald though not from age. Their hair was torn out by cruel hands. I saw this done on two occasions. The lady at the Receiving Cottage who had asked me if I thought myself better than others, as she washed my hair, also asked me another question.

"Would you have protested if I had combed your hair just after combing the head of one covered with sores?"

"This is horrible to me," I answered, "for I have always used my own personal belongings. I would have protested most vehemently."

"But it would not have availed you anything."

Lily Mc:

She was a child of perhaps fifteen years, an Irish beauty, slender but well developed, poised and holding her head proudly. Her hair was long, abundant, fine, naturally curly; black as ebony and shining. Her lovely dark blues eyes were large and expressive, real Irish eyes. Her complexion defied cosmetics, glowing, beautiful red lips and cheeks, a flawless complexion. A laughing voice, for Lily seemed greatly amused by what she saw there.

I wondered how anyone could send such a lovely, proud, ladylike girl to this place. I never knew why, but thought it may have been some schoolgirl love affair which her divorced parents could not control. (For by Lily's prayers later I heard her pray for her father, mother, step father and step mother three times each day.)

This lovely child danced as she walked the first day I saw her when she was brought into the Receiving Cottage. She was so graceful, so sweet. Now months afterward in the second lowest hell, I saw Lily again; but the roses had left her lips and her cheeks. Her bed was near mine and we ate near each other. Three times each day, morning, noon and night, Lily said her prayers audibly, and the proud lady did not say to her, "I'll send you to one of the back wards; I'll put you into a hot pack and lock you up in a padded cell if you don't quit praying." Perhaps they had done that to Lily before she left the Receiving Cottage; but now she was in the lowest hell never complaining, never murmuring. Her slender form was emaciated now; her lovely eyes had lost their sparkle.

Instead they held a look of resignation, as if life were over for her, and it might have been.

"Father, I thank *thee* for this water; I thank *thee* for this bread. Father, I thank *you* for the prunes. I thank *you* for the oatmeal," Lily would pray each mealtime.

Or it would be, "Father, I thank *you* for the cabbage, (or beans). I thank *you* for the potato, (or stew)."

"God bless my mother, God bless my father, God bless my stepmother, God bless my stepfather," she would then say.

Could they know how she was changed? Lily was a slave; a pale, pale lily. No laughter now.

She undoubtedly wore a long, ugly scar under the coarse, rough clothing which she wore as if they were queenly robes. She wore them with such grace. There was no bitterness in her young mind; she was a child of love and sweetness. Lily was ordered to carry those heavy, hard mattresses up to the second floor, a load for a strong man, but she carried them without protest. Also great loads of heavy blankets and hard pillows. She, too, pushed the heavy logs called "polishers" over the floors, morning and evening, as did others including myself when in the Receiving Cottage Lily seemed tireless, going lightly on her slender feet.

I never knew what became of that lovely, pale Lily, who was once an exotic, flaming, glowing blossom. On that first day she came to hell, I saw no one there half so lovely, or more of a lady than she. I prayed much for that child; but never did her parents visit her while I was at that place, and that place may have been the place of her death.

Dances, religious meetings and theatrical plays were all provided for the inmates, each on a different Sunday or Sunday night. I was asked if I wanted to go but refused. I told them I had left that world long before going to hell, by which name I always referred to that place when I spoke of it.

The inmates were dressed in good clothing, probably belonging to others, it did not matter there. Some, were never permitted to wear their clothing or ever see it after they were locked up. The "patients" as they were called, were escorted to these functions by attendants. At those dances the men attendants danced with the women patients; the women attendants danced with the men patients.

Romances often blossomed between women attendants and men patients; even marriages sometimes. As the marriage of the beautiful, proud lady who, the next year, married a man who was in hell for cure of the drink habit.

When relatives or friends came to visit the unfortunates, the attendants dressed them nicely, fixed their hair, and faces were powdered and rouged. They were led out of their cells, taken out of strait jackets and with arms of attendants around them, they were called, in honeyed accents, "darling" and "dear." It may have been just minutes before that they had been kicked and beaten and called almost every horrible and mean epithet. This I knew, for I saw and heard it for myself; but many other things which happened there were talked over by attendants and "trusties." The gossip which went on continually.

These inmates were never left alone with their family or friends and never permitted to speak anything derogatory of that place. When visitors came, if the person they came to visit was beaten up too badly, or in a hot pack, the visitors were told that person was "disturbed" and could not be seen. This I also knew, having seen it done many times. But these relatives had been told that they could visit before coming to the ward. Some came many miles with gifts, but those for whom they were intended never received them.

Visitors were received at the Administration Building first, and then sometimes had to wait hours before being escorted to the wards. The words of Jesus tell us of "white sepulchres;" truly you can find the whited sepulchres in numbers in hell.

"You are here to be cured," the inmates were always told.

That is what they also told me, but I said:

"I am not a patient. I am not ill. I am a prisoner."

Jesus said, *"Be ye wise as serpents and harmless as doves."* Matthew 10:16. There were many serpents in hell and a few doves among the attendants.

A middle-aged woman:

I never heard the woman's name spoken. She evidently was one of the constipated ones, and must have been there a long time, never to be released. She suffered much, and had a revolting habit of using her fingers to dig out her feces to eat. That was one way those depraved creatures had to satisfy their starving bodies. She seemed to like me for she was always trying to get those filthy, encrusted fingers on my face or hands.

Imagine being locked in a small space with such things trying to touch you, and you trying to get away all the time. Yet, trying not to offend the poor insane creature. Always, I went behind someone else, then when she came to the other side of that one moving and continuing to move, until the call to eat or to walk around the circle.

And she went to the table with those terrible hands!

Think of being bathed in a tub, not even rinsed out, after bathing things like that! Think of having to sit opposite such a creature and watch her handle the food bowls that all of us depended on for food! When she could reach any bowls near me, I did not eat. It was too nauseating, yet could I complain or say I wanted to be moved to some other ward? No, I would not have been moved to another place, and if it had been so, it would have contained others like her.

There is no escape in hell, and no escape from hell for us, but Jesus Christ, our *father's name*. That *holy name* kept me in hell and took James and me out of hell and into heaven.

Oh, the cruelty of hell! The monotony of hell!

Men outside in the world are always comparing everything with hell, but there is no comparison. Here is something which tries to describe hell, but it cannot be half told, no more can the wondrous things of heaven ever be half told. We can know them through obedience to *his* great *name*. Here is a poem about hell:

AND WHAT IS HELL?

You will hear men say as they stand on the street
And talk over times gone by, and tales of their troubles tell
Speak of the weather in such a way and say,
    "It's as hot as hell."

You will hear men say at their work or play
When weather is cold and frost rings like a bell,
As they clap their hands and stamp their feet,
    "It's cold as hell."
One will say of his horse, of his partner (or wife
Who spends all his money and in strife and inharmony dwell),
"You know I have a heck of a wife, she's just as tricky as hell."

The medicine as it is measured out by physician
To cure his pains, to help him and make him well,
He will say as he shrugs to swallow it,
    "It's just as bitter as hell."

The boy as he bites the apple so green
Feels the pucker of mouth and tongue, so with a yell,
Cries, "Away with such apples, it's as sour as hell."

The man who for hire the vinegar makes
Or the winery or still which he hides in the dell,
Will say with a smile to his smirking friends,
    "It's as strong as hell."

The girl gone astray from the level way
Bound by sin and its woeful spell,
Will say in her anguish and in her despair,
    "This life is as cruel as hell."

The boy who plays with the baseball and bat
Was struck by the ball as it fell,
Cries in his pain to the other boys,
    "That ball is as hard as hell."

O! Hell is so common and all people compare their
Woes and their joys with hell;
It's a measure they use without knowledge or sense,
For nothing compares with hell.
Take all of the pain and all of the woe,
All of the sorrow and care,
All of life's pleadings and all of life's despair,
All of the heat and all of the cold,
All of the dross and all of the gold,
All of the anguish and all of the sin, all of the mockery,
All of the din and strife of the ages all rolled into one,
And add to it hunger, war, fire, floods and death;
Hell cannot be measured, its depths are too great,
Deeper than the sea and stronger than fate,
More cruel than the grave and hotter than hate.

Why not speak of heaven where God's joys abound?
Why continue to think hell is under the ground?

One woman, then about fifty-five years old, told me that she was brought there twenty-five years before, a young mother of a son, and the wife of a young man.

"They have never visited me in all these years," she said.

She was one of the slaves who seemed to be in possession of sanity, but she told me the most diabolical story, which seems unbelievable but was supposed to have taken place in hell where all kinds of horrible practices are known and practiced.

This is what she told me:

"The doctors take young women who are free from disease, who have just finished menstruating; then they siphon the pure blood from the victim's uterus, and mingle it with wine and drink it. This makes the victim bloodless; very pale, so that they die quickly."

I thought of little pale Lily Mc.

"Who told you this terrible thing?" I asked her.

"The women who were told by these girls themselves."

I have never said that I believe it, but can I say it is not true? It will be known in the last analysis.

That is one of the things that make one shudder with horror.

In the second lowest hell, as I lay on the floor at night, next to me lay the mattress of a young colored woman, weighing about three hundred pounds. I was told that she had killed a woman with a heavy night vessel. Never did I see this woman lying down. She wore a heavy cord circle around both wrists, which she could have taken off because it was about two feet in circumference. But I never saw her without it. Did she think she had handcuffs on her wrists?

While I lay on that bed I never slept but closed my eyes just so I could see through a slit in my eyelids. For this woman stared at me, never seeming to move her eyes from my face. Never did I see her talking to anyone, never did I hear her speak a word. Her face was very sad, and I seemed not to fear her as I lay quietly on that mattress on the floor. I did not speak of her to anyone; it would have been no use to speak of her there. But I was sorry for her, for she was a slave working hard all day in one of the factories.

I had been a good slave there too, until that first day of September when I ceased to work for them in hell. Then on my entrance to this second lowest hell, I stated my position to the nurses.

"I cannot wait on the sick anymore."

"Aren't you ashamed not to wait on them? She asked me. "Aren't you sorry for them?"

"I am not ashamed for what I cannot do, and I am sorrier for them than I can say. However I am not to blame for their being here," I answered.

But since the first of September, the nurses and attendants tried to shame me into doing what I had so gladly done for a long time, and would still have been glad to do if my *heavenly father* had not told me:

"Labor not for the meat that perisheth." John 6:27.

I knew it did not mean the ill and suffering ones, but it did mean for the ones in power over and over them. Also I knew it was not pity for those unfortunates which caused them to revile me, but because I had saved them so much work being quick, intelligent, and doing all they asked me well.

So I steadfastly refused to do any more work in hell, not counting the cost to myself, not knowing what my fate might be because of my refusal to do what they asked of me.

Any sane person would know it is better to be occupied, for work would help that slow, seemingly unending time to go faster. What did it mean to sit unmoving, looking always into faces bereft of reason, watching people suffer agonies of pain, hearing cries of agony and despair? Curses of demonical fury, shrieks of fear, just bearing it and keeping quiet. Thirsting, hungering, bereft of loved ones, in hell as I knew I was and as I believed to die; yet so calm and so at peace, with my mind *"kept by the power of God unto salvation."* Peter 1:5.

Jimmy Kelly:

Jimmy was an alcoholic there for the "cure." Everyone liked Jimmy; he had very blue eyes and a friendly smile. His smile made his face like sunshine. He hauled food in a big cart to the different wards and cottages. There one of the women attendants "fell" for Jimmy, so she told me one day.

"Oh, I have fallen so many times!" she then said.

She was trying to get me to tell her, I knew, of similar experiences. For my story had gone to every dark hole in hell, and I was set apart as a wicked woman. I had nothing to tell the woman as she confessed to me:

"At eleven o'clock last night, I met Jimmy and unlocked the outside gate and set him free."

She was always singing, "Anybody here seen Kelly? Kelly with the blue, blue eyes."

They did not get Jimmy back and I don't think they cared, for there were plenty more to haul the food and do the work he did there. For new ones were coming every day the chariot arrived.

But blue-eyed Jimmy did not live long. I am thankful that he did not die in hell, to be buried in the "peach orchard." That was the way they buried the poor at that place and Jimmy was poor. His body would have been sewed in a sheet and buried in a hole in the ground, dug in the peach orchard. That is the way they buried the unwanted, unloved dead. Jimmy was loved by many people there and he had friends in the outside world. I hope they made his last hours as pleasant as they could.

Regina:

One of the dear, persecuted ones, Regina, like many others, came to me because they felt my love for them; the love God had given me for all suffering humanity. She told me that her priest had put her there years before.

One day Regina gave me a lovely poem which she said she had just written. It is a beautiful prayer and belongs in this book. When later, Regina heard that I was going home she cried:

"You will forget all about us when you are gone."

"No," I promised. "I will never forget you."

She lives in my memory and the poem shall live in this book for many to read and love. I do not know if Regina was ever released from that prison, but I do know that she was one of God's suffering little ones; and that she is safe with *him* whom she loves so much.

REGINA'S PRAYER

Jesus, hear me while I pray. Guide my footsteps
    when I stray;
Send me, Lord, *thy* grace divine, make my heart
    like unto *thine*.
Let me, Lord, *thy* sorrow know. Let me feel
    Thy bitter woe.
Show me, Lord, the nails, the wood. Let me stand
    where *thou* hast stood.
Let my bosom feel the dart, show me the wound—
    Thy bleeding heart.

Let me kiss *thy* feet, *thy* hands, the thorny crown,
    the cruel bands.
Show me *thy way, thy holy will*, the path that leads
    to Calvary's hill.
I would *thy* mercy, Lord, entreat, beside the cross embrace
    Thy wounded feet.
And kneeling on the sacred mount, cleanse my soul in
    Thy red fount.
And hear *thy* last expiring cry, and then, my *Savior*,
    let me die.
Jesus, hear me when I pray; lead me, guide me,
    when I stray.

                                    —*My Prayer, by Regina C.*

Some weeks after being sent to the second lowest hell, I was told that efforts were being made on my behalf for my release. When I was told this by one who had some authority there, I asked that my husband, James, be released with me.

"No," I was told, "one of you must stay."

In the beginning we had been told, "Neither of you will ever get out of here." Now it was, "One of you must stay."

I thought of the tender little babe who needed me so much. I knew that a father, no matter how kind and loving, could never take the place of a mother; for I had lost my own precious mother at a very early age and spent a lonely and unhappy childhood. I knew that if it was my *heavenly father's will*, I would go to my little son.

Through all this terrible experience I had never doubted God, although nothing had occurred as I thought it would. But he said, *"For my thoughts are not your thoughts; neither are your ways my ways,"* Isaiah 55:8. I did not yet understand my *heavenly father's thoughts* or *his ways*, but was beginning to learn that they were not literal as I had

believed and had obeyed as I believed, and so went blindly
to hell for that belief which I soon knew was wrong. For no
one can understand the Bible but by the *spirit* which spoke
through Jesus. I learned that none of the things I had literally
believed of the blessed hidden *words* were real, just shad-
ows like a mirage; a covering for the *word* as the husk covers the wheat.

"If I have to go without James, I'll be leaving half of my
heart here."

But I knew not what I spoke, for I did not know that we
two were the only ones who had been called to go through
this terrible place for *his name* that we might be accounted
worthy. As we had suffered shame for *his name* to bring back
to the world what had been hidden for centuries of years, the
salvation of the lost world.

Then the good doctor spoke to me of my pending release.

"I will not go unless my husband tells me to go," I said
to him.

"Write him a note and I will deliver it to him, and bring
you an answer."

The next day he brought the note from James.

"Go, my dear wife, and God go with you."

On the day before I had asked the doctor if he could
arrange for us to see and talk with each other before I was
sent away.

"I will do what I can," he promised.

In a few days James was brought into the visiting room
of the second lowest hell, and I was taken there to meet him.

"Just ten minutes," ordered the two men who brought
James.

They did not leave us alone during the "just ten minutes,"
but many were in the room and passing in and out.

That mattered not to us.

We kissed each other, we sat side by side, we held each others hands and we talked of the blessed things of God.

"I will come and join you as soon as I can," James said bravely.

But he knew they had told us they never intended to let him go while life was in his body.

"I will never stop trying to get you free until you are free," I said.

And I kept that promise; working, praying, seeking.

Thinking it might be the last time, those ten minutes were swiftly gone. Then a "God bless you" from one to the other, and "God keep you" from one to the other. His blue eyes were filled with tears as we kissed goodbye. My eyes were wet too, but on his face was a look of courage and determination. Sadness was in my heart, because as I had told the *father* in heaven, James would not be in hell had not I told him about the *fathers' name*.

God said to me in that sweet, still *voice*:

"The reward he shall receive will far outweigh his sufferings here, it will be so much greater."

It was only ten minutes, but we did get to be together!

Alone with God, though surrounded by many who watched us every minute. We did not care, for we talked in the language of heaven, though it was our own language called English. We breathed together that foul, fetid air. Just ten minutes granted us for what seemed ages of cruel suffering.

He was the first man to believe the *revelation* God gave me of *his name* Jesus Christ. That seemed so long ago! What were man-made marriages, made and broken, to the marriage of the *spirit* which could not be broken? But I was soon to learn by that *spirit*, that now the law of our land must be obeyed in the marriage by the law. Still I thought, "What are man-made marriages and man-made laws to the *law* of God?"

I knew that God had and has a great *salvation* for the world, who forgot God, and must be brought back to *him*. You know, as I know, that many have been persecuted and denied, even called crazy as was for example Columbus, who died in chains. Yet, who is there in the world today who believes this earth we live on is flat and square? What about our great men to whom God gave minds which changed our meager lives and gave us luxurious and wonderful things not even dreamed of? God gave these gifts for humanity to have, to enjoy. But what denials and persecutions were met by those to whom *he* gave the minds to produce them!

The greatest *gift* of God, *his son*, is rejected, denied *his father's name*; that *name* being uttered in curses on the lips of degraded men and women, also ignorantly spoken by swearing men and women—even little children. God's *son*, not a man or a woman, not a physical child of human beings or origin, but a *body of words*, a *spiritual body* containing *spirit* and *life*.

You will read about these things in John's *gospel*, which is not John's but Jesus Christ's the *father's*.

These *words*, spoken through the lips of a man born of Joseph the carpenter and of Mary his wife, himself also a carpenter, working with his father at their trade until called to preach at the age of thirty years. There is no doubt that Mary believed as I did, until I learned better by the *revelation* of God after suffering, that the little body of human flesh born to her and Joseph months after she had been told she should bring forth a son, was mistaken for the *son* of God.

"How shall these things be?" Mary asked, because she was a woman, a natural woman as I was when years before my little son was born, I was told the same words that were spoken to her.

How many other women here believed that they would become the mother of Jesus? Perhaps countless thousands.

"Oh, we've had many women here who believed they were to give birth to the *son* of God," many nurses told me in that hell.

I asked them, "But did they have a man here at the same time?" A man who believed as the woman believed?"

"No, never any man," they would then admit.

My *heavenly father* knew that we were without understanding of the *scriptures*, but we did not know the meaning was hidden deep in them and there was no one who knew. There was none to tell us the *truth* so God took a way to mold that knowledge in us. A way unforgettable and glorious, after *he* had finished *his* work in us, *his* two blind and deaf children delivered to the slaughter.

Now there is no need for men or women to be deceived into believing that human beings can, or will, or ever did bring forth the *son* of God but by way of the *mind* of God; which *he* gave to Mary and Joseph long ago, which *he* gave to James and me for this age.

For "*In the beginning was the word. And the word was God.*" That *word* was made *flesh*; that *flesh* lived in the mind of the son of Mary and Joseph; not human flesh, but *words*. The *flesh* of the *word* is *words*. Tell them they must eat that *flesh*, which is *words* of God, spoken by the mouth of Jesus, and drink that *blood*, which is the understanding of those *words*, as John 6:53.

Had we known the meaning of the *scriptures* as we know now, as we have known for years, we would not have had to suffer in hell. But the true *church* (the *Saviour* was in the minds of these) was put to death in every conceivable manner of torture, and no one left of those who knew the *truth* and *life* of God. No one to teach us how to obey both God and man. There is no resurrection in hell, the place of death, for no *life* of God can be brought forth there. The resurrection and *life* did not come to James and me while in hell, but after my deliverance from that place of terror.

The arrangements for my release were all made, when the day of freedom, November 4th, arrived at last. One of the nurses told me that I would have to sign a paper before I could leave the place. A paper which said that I had received nothing but kind treatment and good care.

"I will not sign it," I said to her, "for I will not sign a lie."

Tears began to course down her cheeks; for she was very fond of me, as were the others on that last ward.

"Then you will never get out of here," she cried through her tears.

"Well, I still will not sign it."

And in a few moments I walked through the office alone. No one was in the office. No paper was presented to me to sign.

I was free!

*The darkness of ignorance—within the walls of the
asylum, in secret, patients were deprived of every
freedom, human right and decency.*

Part VI
FREEDOM AND LIBERTY

1776 - LIBERTY - 19__

In a prison at dreary midnight
She ran to the prison bars
And gazed into the heavens
With its great mass of stars;
A great bell swung high before her
Its tongue a *message* pealed
Liberty!!! The *name* it uttered
No other was *revealed*.

It passed and on a throne
A man and a woman stood
A white babe on her bosom
The badge of motherhood;
A change came o'er the baby
Enhanced an hundred-fold
It changed to a snowy lily
With a heart of purest gold.

Months passed and came the tidings
Of a wondrous iron bell
Liberty the name they gave it
All the country loved it well;
When our country was in bondage
Glorious tidings it did bring
When the voice came pealing
In the night, ring, ring, ring!
But oh, the wondrous pity
Its glorious voice was gone
It was coming to the city
This dear old silent bell;
And a woman watched and waited
Hoping liberty it would tell
As the vision in the prison
In that dreary midnight cell.

The day dawned bright and sunny
Bells rang and whistles blew
Thousands stood and waited
The famous bell to view;
And out to a cheerless prison
A message sped away
For one the barred doors opened
On this very glorious day.

To the old historical city
The bell had come and gone
Its work in that city finished
Its mission there was done;
Among the trains leaving the city
One carried the old iron bell
Another carried two chastened hearts
Who the story of Christ will tell.

FREEDOM AND LIBERTY

The old conveyance containing a doctor and nurse waited for me outside. They escorted me to the train a number of miles from hell, made sure I got on, and watched me leave. Waiting at the end of that journey on the train was my son and the kind friend who had taken care of him for those long months.

Oh, how happy I was to see my little son again!

My friend loved him so much she did not like to give him up, but she knew that I had suffered bitterly to hold him again, and he was my son, my little beloved. I eagerly took him into my arms and hugged him close to my aching heart. How wonderful it was to hold him, to kiss his soft cheek, to touch his golden curls, to feel his little hand in mine.

On the rest of the trip to my friend's home, my baby sat upon my lap, soberly looking at me without a smile. He was too white! He had grown and changed greatly, and for the moment I was a stranger to him. He did not know his mother, perhaps he never will know me as I am, filled with longing to save my darling from every hurt, from every evil and harmful thing. But my *heavenly father* knows my baby's mother's heart, and the heart of his father, then still imprisoned in a horrible place we know is hell.

After a few days, I located our own living quarters for my son and myself.

But I was an outcast.

Only my *heavenly father* knows the storms, the piercings of the thorns I walked upon with tired feet. All the blasts of hell's fury seemed to have been unleashed against me, so helpless and separated from my beloved James.

I had no friends, but the one kind couple who had stood by us. Even so, it was necessary for me to work to pay rent and buy food for baby and myself. Wages were very poor, so my living was not much but it was clean. And I was free!

At every opportunity I went to different religious groups, hoping to ask their prayers for James's release; but they refused me entrance to their places of worship. It is where Mammon is worshiped but God is unknown there. Always I took my lovely baby with me wherever I went.

Then one day I went to see the handsome judge who said to me, that long-ago day, "committed," without a trial. The judge who pronounced that awful fate upon us. We expected punishment but not that! He sat in his large and comfortable chair in his office, and asked me to be seated in the chair before him. I held my lovely baby on my lap. Steadily my son looked at the judge without smiling as though he knew it was he who had been the instrument used in our punishment.

The judge watched the baby, then spoke.

"You have a fine son."

But I didn't go there to talk of my son, so I quickly told him my errand was to have him get my husband free from that terrible place to which he had sent us.

"You did not give us a chance," I said. "You did not hear our story. You gave us no trial."

"I did many things when I sat in that chair that have troubled my conscience ever since," he said. "I will go there in February and get your husband released. I am sure when I ask it will be granted.

But in February the judge did not go and I do not believe he ever went. In February his wife died, and I did not go to see him ever again because he did not keep his word.

When nine months had passed sadly and slowly for me and for James, after my deliverance, he finally obtained permission for me to visit him. I went, taking our darling, then fifteen months old, talking and running on swift little feet. His head held high, he walked into the doctors' offices, large blue eyes shining, little red mouth smiling, unafraid in hell because there was no evil in the mind of the little babe. But his sweet innocence was unnoticed by the doctors as if he did not exist.

On this first visiting day, I asked the superintendent to give my husband his freedom, but he answered me as he always did when I visited James:

"He is the most insane man here."

A lie, and he knew it was a lie, as I did.

"Do you still hear voices?" he then asked me.

"No," I answered. "I never heard voices, only as you or anyone else speaks. The *voice* of God is inaudible."

He made no answer.

From the superintendent's office I took my little son to the visiting room. No one led me; free to walk, but only to see our loved one when they chose to grant us that short visiting hour in the presence of nurses, attendants and other visitors and their unfortunates whom they came to visit.

And then, there was James at last. What a happy, but at the same time sorrowful reunion we three had that day in hell.

Frugally, I saved that I might go as often as possible to see my baby's father, my dear, true husband. When I went, including the first time, I always took something for the three of us to eat, and ate with him there. Strangely, no one objected, so, James had clean and wholesome, though meager, food on those occasions. Always we thanked our *heavenly father* for *his* loving care, for every blessing.

Every trip I asked the superintendent for James's release and met refusal, curt and hard, and the cruel words with which he had answered me at the first visit. The horrors of hell weighed heavily on James, but he did not talk of those things when we were together. James told me many precious *scriptures* he had learned during those long hours, days, weeks, months and then years of our separation.

Constantly I tried in the only way I could know, to obtain James's release, but failing until God should make a way for his freedom. Always when we visited just that one short hour, no matter if I were there two or even three hours before, I could only see him at their own time and not my desire to spend more time with him. When that door was locked behind baby and me, there was no going back for a last kiss or words of "goodbye."

Our little son soon learned to ask me to "Go see Papa, twain?" Every day he wanted to go on the train to see Papa. However, I could only afford to go once each month at the first, but in the last year of his imprisonment I obtained more work and went oftener, and then every two weeks. But we could never be alone. Always many walked and talked there, but we talked not of ourselves but of the *words* of God. Seeking always to know *his will* for us to do.

When our Lord by *spirit* and *words* showed me that I must obey the law in marriage and he with me, James could not see it until our Lord also *revealed* it to him. When he did understand it was God's *will,* he too then asked the superintendent that we might marry and he be free to care for his family.

At his offer to comply with the law in marriage, nearly all the doctors came asking him questions.

"Who changed you? What happened to you that you make this offer now?" they all asked.

"No one but God could change my mind."James answered truthfully.

On leaving from my next visit after James told them his decision, the superintendent stopped me.

"What did you tell James to change him? What happened?"

"No," I said, "I could not change him; I did not change him. Only God could change him."

"Well, we are going to put your husband to the test now. If he will work for us ten days we will give him his liberty."

I knew that no man ever worked harder than James in that place until we were both told the same thing and on the same day, *"Labor not for the meat that perisheth."* John 6:27.

Our work there was finished!

On that occasion the authorities, in order to intimidate James and make him do their will instead of God's *will,* put him in the lowest hell where he had not been before. There he was locked in that barred place with men who had committed murder and other crimes. These madly insane inmates beat and killed each other, constantly tearing and destroying themselves and unwary guards in ferocious fights. These men who had lost all semblance to humans, circled James and sniffed at his clothes, as wild animals would do, but never did they touch him. God kept him.

To this ward two guards or attendants came together for protection, and always armed with guns and clubs, for they feared the prisoners.

James was kept in that place three days, but being removed each night and taken back to the same ward he was taken from in the morning. During these three days James sat in the midst of those poor creatures and read his Bible all day long; at night he slept soundly in the company of more made men in the first ward.

It is written, *"He giveth his beloved sleep."* Psalm 127:2.

So soundly did James sleep, that one night during his stay in hell, someone stole his Bible from under his pillow, and keeping it one day, returned it under his pillow the next night. But I had scarcely slept in hell, never soundly; perhaps because I, being a mother, had too much care on my mind for my son, both before and after his birth.

At the end of the third day, when James was taken out of the murderer's ward, his mind not broken, the attendants questioned him.

"Where do you want us to take you?'

But James was not to be misled by their question; he knew that no one ever got what they asked for there.

"You are running this place. I have not anything to say. That is your business," he answered.

So James was taken to the ward where he slept and never again removed to the lowest hell. Neither could they force him to work after that first day of September, as I also had refused.

Now at the end of the visiting day, as I stood and heard the superintendent's words, "If James will work for us ten days we will give him his liberty," my flesh shook on my bones for the awful fear that in his longing to be free, James might consent to their demand. That then we should never meet again. That door was locked behind me; there was no going back because they would not permit it. I could not write to warn him; our letters were opened and read before we saw them. (In that place letters were brought to me by the proud lady, very wet from the steam to get them unsealed.) I knew that all James's letters to me after I was away were read before they were sent.

In agony of soul I left there praying, that was all I could do, that God would show James what to do before morning came.

God answered that prayer, which I prayed many times day and night as the long days went by until my next trip and I saw him again.

"My very flesh shook on my bones," I told James "for fear that you, in your desire to be free, would answer them before you knew God's *will* in this matter. I longed so for you to be free to come to us, your little son and I need you so."

"I asked the Lord what to do. When they came that morning and told me, 'If you will work for us ten days we will set you free,' my answer was ready. One of the attendants had told me ahead what they would ask me to do, that they would give me my liberty if I would work ten days for them. But the Lord spoke to me about 2:30 in the morning.

'You may take your choice; refuse to work for them and I will set you free, or go to work for them and you will never have your liberty.'

So when the superintendent told me his proposition, my decision was ready.

'No, I am through working here,' I told him. 'Did the *father* say to the *prodigal son* on his return, 'Go and work ten days.'? I would not work for you ten minutes to get my liberty. You know that I can work and you know that I should not be held here in this place. I have told you what I would do, that I would be married by the law; I have asked forgiveness of you for breaking your law. But instead of forgiving me you tell me, 'Go and work for us ten days and we will set you free.'"

Then the attendants took James to the basement and stood him up against a wall of that hideous place after he steadfastly refused to work for them.

"Don't you know that we have the power to kill you?" they threatened.

"Go ahead and do all you have a mind to do," James answered, "for I was never more ready to lose this body of flesh and bones than I am now."

The men wilted and could not lay hands on him, and no one ever did all that dreadful time in hell. Then they took him back to his ward. But instead of forgiving and releasing James when he declared his intention of upholding man's law in marriage, their only reason for our incarceration, he was kept locked up for another long, seemingly interminable fifteen months.

On one of my visits toward the last, James gave me the address of his relatives whom I did not know and had never met.

"Will you write to my sister?" he asked. "Tell her I can no longer live in this place. Ask her if she will try to have me released."

Gladly I accepted this proposal to write to his relatives, and on reaching the place where baby and I lived and I worked, I wrote that very night, for it was always late when we arrived.

Soon I received a reply to my letter. James's sister sent the address of his brother and she said:

"Write to him, maybe we two together can get James free."

So letters went back and forth between James's relatives and me. Their letters I took with me and read to him on my visits with him. We both began to hope for his release, that now God's *will* be done.

And then the three years were past.

The superintendent told James's brother, "He's got to be out of here by the fifteenth of this month."

I was told the glad news and obtained money for fare for us that we might go to a place where we could live together after we were joined in marriage by law. Every arrangement was made. I gave money to James's brother to buy the tickets for us on the train. The only money the brother provided was for a cheap suit of clothes which I asked him to get for James.

That night, November 15th, James walked through the superintendent's office, not signing any paper as I had not signed any. No one questioned him, and from that moment he was free! Free to join us on that train, free to make a home for us, free to worship and serve God, but although given his natural liberty, hated and despised by the world which "professed" to love Jesus.

No welcome for us in the camps of the so-called Christian world. But we love all the worlds our God created and are willing to "lay down" our life for them, as the *good shepherd* lay down *his life* for the sheep. We knew that our Lord had purged our souls of all uncleanness of the world's many forms of religion, all its misunderstandings and sins. We also learned there was no liberty for us until those people had extracted the fullness of their pleasure in *his* sufferings. But James and I have forgiven everything that was done to us; long years ago we forgave them who refused to forgive us.

Now we could go on, saddened by the hardness of heart of people who profess to love God.

At the time of James's release, he, baby and I went to the place designated on our tickets, first obtaining a marriage license and having the marriage between us performed by a judge in a town where the train made a stop of a few hours. That did not change us, but now the law which we had out-raged, according to men, was or should have been satisfied. But if God had not shown us to obey that law after obedience to *him*, we could not or would not have done so. If others will hear us, they will never take the way that we were compelled to take to find the *way* of *life* through God's *great name*.

A man found it.

It is not any more to be found that way of hell.

On the train I held my lovely golden baby in my arms. My golden haired son! I looked into his large blue eyes with their black lashes, so long, thick and upcurled, and whis-pered to him.

"My own precious little angel, our *heavenly father* is watching over you. You have a sad destiny, my darling, for all the world hates your father and mother because we had to take a way they do not understand. We had to find the hidden things of God as *he* purposed us to do."

Was he too tiny to understand? Perhaps so, but he may have understood things he could not speak.

I knew that a great *salvation* was near for the world whose rulers and teachers "forgot God" and had left *him* out of their counsels. That world must be brought back to *him*. This was the greatest of all, the bringing back to the begin-ning, from the sins of the world, God's people filled with *his* blessed knowledge. Not to be joined unequally, but by *his spirit* and by the law; a perfect *law* so there will be no more sorrow, no more sin, no more divorces.

No one can express the riches of God's *pardon, his peace*, which is free to all who will, in true repentance, come and partake of the *gift* of *his holy name*, Jesus Christ. There will be no need for hospitals, jails, insane hospitals (hell), penitentiaries, when there are no sick, no insane, no transgression of the law, no wars, for they shall cease.

God's *promises* are *true*, and there is no power above *his great name*, the half which cannot be told is *revealed*.

A few years after my release, I met a physician whom I had known for years, one who seemed to be a good friend of my family. I told him of the practices in that most awful place called a "mental hospital." He had said long ago, "I like for you to care for my patients, for you pray for them and they always recover." But on this day when I told him of those seven women fed by that horrible method with a tube not washed, he yelled at me, "I don't believe it!" But it is true and I told him so.

"It is true. What object could I have in telling a lie against anyone? I live for God who delivered my husband and me from that hell."

Still he said angrily he did not believe it. No matter if people refuse to believe what I saw and know was done there, I would be sorry for them to have the experience of it in order to know.

No matter how the world despises us, hates us, shuns us, our Lord suffered the hatred, the scorn, and was despised before they hated us.

"Ye shall be hated of all men for my name's sake," Mark 13:13.

Men have not believed the *scriptures* of the King James orthodox Bible, but I know *them* and know *they* are true.

All these Bibles of spurious origin are made by unbelievers to sell, to make a profit, to turn away the people from the *true* and *living* God, Jesus Christ. *Beware of them who are wearing the clothing of sheep* (the *words* of Jesus) *but inwardly they are murderers, hypocrites, and liars*, Matthew 7:15

"Cease *from man whose breath is in his nostrils*," Isaiah 2:22. Lift up Jesus Christ from the earth, from looking at God as a man, a human being! Then you will know that no mortal woman or man could be used as vessels to contain the "body" of God's *only begotten son*—only in their minds. For God is a *spirit* and *his only begotten son* is a *body of words*, which was made *flesh* in the mind of the mortal son or human child born to Mary and Joseph.

But that "*holy thing*" called Immanuel (God with us) was not the son of either Mary or Joseph. When you "*eat the flesh of the son of man, and drink his blood*" John 6:53, you will know that *flesh* is the *word* spoken by the man who was called Jesus.

"Thou shalt call *his name* Jesus." As Mary and Joseph called their son, and as I called my son because I could not understand even as Joseph and Mary could not understand. Mary brought forth a human body, called Jesus, whose mind contained the *body* of *words* and spoke them which is, was and ever shall be "*the word of God, his only begotten son.*"

Deny it if you can, but if you believe the *scriptures*, if you accept the only "*name under heaven given among men whereby we must be saved*" (Jesus Christ) Hebrews 13:8, you will know it is the *name* of the only *true* and *living* God. There is no escape for you if you deny *his holy name*.

Someone met the cruel, the unspeakable punishment of hell, to know the *truth* of the *scriptures*, that you and all this world may be saved from all the delusions and mistakes, the sins, the hates and crimes of adultery, murders and wars.

Repent and believe the gospel!

Repent and be *baptized* in the *name* of Jesus Christ *(the name of the father and of the son and of the holy ghost—one name)*, hidden in Matthews 28:19 and other *scriptures*. Search the *words* of Jesus. Search the *prophets* and the *psalms*.

As it is written, First Corinthians 2:9, *"Eye hath not seen nor ear heard, neither have entered into the heart of man the things which God hath prepared for them that love him." But God hath revealed them unto us by his spirit, for the spirit searcheth all things, yea the deep things of God.*

Eye hath not seen—because it is not written; it is *revealed*.

Ear hath not heard—because it is spoken in an inaudible *voice*.

Neither hath entered into the heart of man—because the heart of man in deceitful above all things, and is desperately wicked. Jeremiah 17:9.

Ezekial 11:19, *"And I will take the stony heart out of their flesh and will give them an heart of flesh."*

Ezekial 16:26, *"A new heart also will I give you, and a new spirit will I put within you; and I will take the stony heart out of your flesh and I will give you an heart of flesh." That heart of "flesh" is the gift of God's only begotten son, the word that "was made flesh."*

John 6:53, *"Except ye eat the flesh of the son of man (words of Jesus) and drink his blood, ye have no life in you."*

Then stop your abominations and "do *his commandments!*"

That *word* was never made human flesh, but was manifested through the mouth of a man, born of a man and woman known as Joseph and Mary. *that heart* of *flesh* has all things of God to give to them who love God.

"Ask and ye shall receive. Seek and ye shall find. Knock and it shall be opened unto you." Matthew 7:7.

How shall you ask? "Ask of God which giveth abundantly and upbraideth not." "Hitherto, ye have asked nothing in *my name*."

Seek "in the *way*," the *words* of Jesus. "*Heaven and earth shall pass away but my words shall not pass away*." Search the *scriptures*—John 5:39.

How shall ye seek? Matthew 6:33, "*Seek ye first the kingdom of God and his righteousness*."

How shall you knock? Before it is too late and not as they who say, "Lord, Lord" and do not *his will*. Do not knock when the *door* is shut.

Believe the *words* of that man who said, "*To this end was I born and for this cause came I into the world, that I might bear witness to the truth*." John 18:37. Who also said, "*Why do you go about to kill me, a man who has told you the truth, which I have heard of God?*" John 8:40.

Believe! Repent! And be *baptised*, not by, through or into any water, but into the *word* of Jesus—*the water of life*. "*It shall be in you a well of water, springing up into everlasting life!*" John 4:14.

O, wonderful name of God, Jesus Christ!

Jesus said, "*They will not believe, though one rose from the dead*." Luke 16:31. One, nay two, have risen from the dead out of the same hell where Jesus went and preached to "the spirits in prison."

Epilogue

Extracts From Letter Written to a Young Friend

*"Sorry that you cannot reconcile yourself to conform to the **will** of God, through **his son**, which is to abide in **him** and work for the **kingdom** of God. Never was the world of people in a more dangerous condition.*

*The first thing is to teach them the **father's name** and **baptism** in **his name**, not water but the **words** of Jesus, which is the **water** of **life**. Teaching them that no human son born to Mary or any other woman is the **son** of God. The human being can be only a receiving and sending or giving unit. As long as people are kept in darkness, so long will women all over the world believe sincerely that they will be favored as they think Mary was, and the men in the case believe that they will be used to bring conception of the **son** of God, while many of these men believe they are God himself in reality. Such delusions enter the minds of the people because they do not understand the **scriptures** nor the **spirit** which speaks (in their minds) the **scriptures**.*

*I did not know, wherefore came the breaking of the **words** of Jesus to take me to hell and damn me in the sight of a religious (?) world. But having paid the price I do know now and I want all people to be undeceived, so they may have the **victory** of Jesus Christ which I now have. If God in **his** infinite **mercy**, had not permitted me to suffer the penalty of the damned, how could the **truth** and **life** of **his** **son** been made manifest? Been made "alive again" in a dead world?*

I know that many are called "but few are chosen."

*If when all failed for me, I had given up instead of pressing on, the **truth** of God would still have been hidden in the **scriptures**. But throughout my whole life, God prepared me (all unknown to me) to endure hardness, to know that I must go on no matter as though through fire. I do not claim any virtue or strength of my own. He held me, or I should have perished years ago as countless thousands have perished.*

*Now my desire is to write all this experience and have it printed so that all people can see and know the **son** and the **father** also.*

*You take an apple—it is one, yet in it is food and in it is life, (seeds). It also has a covering or skin to cover the food. It is like God—in three parts, yet **one**. His **way** covers the **truth** and the **life** of the **scriptures**.*

*This fight of God is honorable, but all the glory belongs to **him**. Make the inside of the platter and cup clean. The world makes the outside of the cup and platter clean* *(outward appearance of righteousness), but the inside is full of extortion and excess.*

*How is the inside of the cup and platter made clean? "Now ye are clean through the **word** which I have spoken unto you." John 15:3.*

*We have learned the wonderful meaning of the **words**, "This is **my body** which is broken for you." I broke **it** because someone had to and God chose me. He knew that I would never give up until **it** was finished, but I broke **it** in ignorance, not in wilfulness, not knowing why I was being so used. And **he** gave me these **words** years afterwards, "She is forgiven much, because she loved much."*

Thank you, my blessed Lord Jesus.

*Now will you say to our Lord, "Lord, what wilt **thou** have me to do?" You have been taught and you know the **truth**. You will never need to break the **law** of God nor the law of man, which God gave to him.*

A Letter To My Son

"My first-born, you were promised to me three years before you were born and God told me to call your name Jesus. I knew about you even then, three years lacking one month and fourteen days, or on September 17th. I marveled how that could be! Then in May on the 13th day I was told, "In this set time next year Sarah shall bear a son." Then again on September 17th following, again came the promise to me of your birth and name.

Early in the morning of May 3rd the next year, a few min-utes after the end of May 2nd at the midnight hour, I heard a great number of harps playing soft, sweet music. It came nearer until it was in the hall; it filled the place. Mercy, who was there with me heard it too.

"Mercy," I asked her, "do you hear the music?"

"Yes," she answered, "I hear it. It is not earthly music."

At seven in the morning of that third day of May you were born, as beautiful as a pearl without a flaw, your little body was perfect, pearly white. I saw your little body only once, that was the day they let me dress you, the day they let me send you away from hell. They helped me into a chair and drew the chair into the "parlor" where weeks before I had been locked in with needles, thimble and scissors to sew your little garments before you were born.

There in that room, locked in, that Sunday in May, when you were three weeks and one day old, they brought water, soap and towels for me to bathe you. They brought your little clothes for me to put on you. This was the only kind-ness the proud lady ever showed me, but God let me have that consolation. She put you in my longing arms and left us alone after locking the door.

Only that one time did I get to minister to your needs, my darling, except each four hours they brought you to me to nurse. My falling tears helped the water to wash you; my kisses bathed you with love so tender and sorrow-filled. Nothing could have caused me to send you away but the knowledge that you were being tortured to hurt me. That you might be smothered or killed in some other way to appease the anger of the woman who hated me without a cause. You would be with friends who loved you because they loved your father and mother.

The day you were six months and one day old I saw you again and you did not know me. You were thin and your lovely little face looked white. You sat upright on my lap looking into my eyes but you did not know me and you did not smile. My darling I was so grieved for you and so glad to have you at last.

That day in May when you were three weeks old was the last time your sweet baby lips pressed my breast. My darling little son Jesus, you will soon be a man. May your life be as pure and beautiful as your little body was that day of that year in May.

*God chose you before you were ever conceived in the womb of your mother, chosen to be a saviour of your fellow man. Turn your back on all the foolish things, all the evil things, for a "wise son is the glory of his father, but a foolish son is the heaviness of his mother," says the **scripture**. May you, my precious child, fulfill the **will** of God, **his commandments**; "honor thy father and thy mother;" "children, obey your parents in the Lord."*

*Remember God's **words** are **true** and we cannot pass them by. He is my life and **he** gave you to me. You are precious treasure to the Lord and your father, mother and brother.*

Love forever,

Mother

*Dorothy Ramsey aka Grandma Dodie with Grandson
and editor Michael Miller, Thanksgiving 2015.*